TELEVISION

The Edward Carnell Library

*An Introduction to Christian Apologetics,** 1948

Television: Servant or Master, 1950

The Theology of Reinhold Niebuhr, 1951

A Philosophy of the Christian Religion, 1952

*A Christian Commitment,** 1957

*The Case for Orthodox Theology,** 1959

The Kingdom of Love and the Pride of Life, 1960

The Burden of Søren Kierkegaard, 1965

*The Case for Biblical Christianity,** 1969

*These reprint editions also include Edward Carnell's Presidential Inaugural Address, "The Glory of a Theological Seminary," presented at Fuller Seminary in 1955. This appears at the end of these books.

TELEVISION

Servant or Master?

by

EDWARD JOHN CARNELL, TH.D, PH.D.
*Associate Professor of Systematic Theology,
Fuller Theological Seminary, Pasadena, Calif.*

Author of

AN INTRODUCTION TO CHRISTIAN APOLOGETICS

WIPF & STOCK · Eugene, Oregon

Wipf and Stock Publishers
199 W 8th Ave, Suite 3
Eugene, OR 97401

Television
Servant or Master?
By Carnell, Edward John
Copyright©1950 Becker, Jean Carnell and Carnell, John
ISBN 13: 978-1-55635-622-3
ISBN 10: 1-55635-622-6
Publication date 9/18/2007
Previously published by W. MB. Eerdmans Publishing Company, 1950

Foreword

Edward J. Carnell (1919–1967) is one of the most fascinating figures in twentieth-century American evangelicalism. By age forty he had produced a corpus of major writings more impressive than many scholars produce in a far longer lifetime. Nor was he, like some, writing essentially the same book in differing forms. His writing was marked both by creativity and by remarkable development during his relatively short productive career. He was also, by all accounts, the most popular teacher at Fuller Theological Seminary, where he taught from 1948 until 1967 and served as president from 1954 to 1959. For a few years, at the peak of his brief career, he was regarded as the leading intellectual representative of evangelicalism in the larger American theological community. Although his writings are today not as well-known as they were in the past—a regrettable situation that we can hope this volume will begin to remedy—he played a major role in setting the tone for much of future evangelicalism, especially the kind of approach represented these days at Fuller Theological Seminary.

The son of a Baptist pastor, Carnell received his BA from Wheaton College, where he was influenced by the philosopher Gordon H. Clark (1902–1986). Graduating from Wheaton in 1941, Carnell went on to Westminster Theological Seminary where he studied with apologist Cornelius Van Til (1895–1987). In 1944, the same year that Carnell completed his BD at Westminster, Clark and Van Til became engaged in a sharp controversy concerning Clark's more rationalistic apologetic and Van Til's presuppositional approach. Carnell, who sided with Clark, was searching for his own resolution of these differences. He also sought to engage the Protestant intellectual mainstream of the day, going on to Harvard Divinity School for a ThD, where he wrote on Reinhold Niebuhr. While in the Boston area he enrolled in a second doctoral program in philosophy at Boston University. He wrote his doctoral dissertation there on Søren Kierkegaard and received his PhD in 1949. Eventually he turned these works into books on these prominent figures.

More remarkably, while he was engaged in these two doctoral programs, he produced his first major book, *An Introduction to Christian Apologetics*, published in 1948. This volume, which addressed issues that Carnell had been wrestling with in his studies with Clark and Van Til, received the "Evangelical Book Award" of $5,000 (a comfortable year's salary) from William B. Eerdmans Publishing Company.

When in 1948 Carnell took a position at Fuller Theological Seminary in Pasadena, California, he was already established as a prodigy of the "new evangelical" movement that was emerging out of fundamentalism. Fuller Seminary had been founded just the previous year to be the intellectual flagship of this movement. Harold J. Ockenga (1905–1985), pastor of Park Street Church in Boston, was the leader of this movement and served as Fuller Seminary's president *in absentia*. Fundamentalist radio evangelist Charles E. Fuller (1887–1968) provided solid funding. The seminary was to be made up of theological "stars" of the movement and Carnell joined Carl F. H. Henry (1913–2003) as one of the brightest younger lights.

Having accomplished so much before the age of thirty, Carnell had the highest ambitions for the movement of which he was a part and for his role in it. In his efforts to revolutionize evangelical apologetics, he frankly aspired to be the evangelical equivalent of Paul Tillich or Reinhold Niebuhr, the best-known Protestant theologians of the era; he looked to have, as these theologians did, a major national audience. His hopes to be a popular commentator soon met with disillusion when his small book, *Television: Servant or Master?* (1950), despite its balanced approach, proved to be a commercial failure. Nonetheless, his determination to change the face of the theological world remained intact.

In 1952 he published a second major work on apologetics, *A Philosophy of the Christian Religion*. In this he departed from his earlier emphasis on the law of non-contradiction and "systematic consistency" and emphasized more that Christianity best satisfied the heart's desire for meaningful values. Five years later, in 1957, he published a third apologetic work, *Christian Commitment: An Apologetic*, this time with a major commercial publisher, Macmillan in New York. Addressing Christianity's "cultured despisers," this highly original volume emphasized the existential appeal of Christianity. Particularly Carnell emphasized the commonalities between the experiences of believers and non-believers and how Christianity best accounts for universal moral sentiments, such as moral outrage or a sense of injustice. The book, although creative, did not have the impact that Carnell hoped. Part of the problem was that Carnell, despite his immense intelligence, was less and less working within a tradition. Béla Vassady, a distinguished Reformed theologian from Hungary who was briefly a colleague of Carnell, later commented that he was amazed at the degree Carnell believed he could reconstruct Christian thought on his own. Theologian John G. Stackhouse Jr. has suggested that Carnell was a sort of "intellectual Thoreau," depending on insights into his own experience and then generalizing to all humanity. These perceived traits may help to explain why Carnell did not gain a larger public constituency.

In the meantime Carnell had been elevated to the presidency of Fuller Theological Seminary where he encountered some other problems. In May 1955 he delivered his inaugural address, "The Glory of a Theological Seminary." In it he emphasized the need for mutual tolerance and for emphasizing Christian love over fine points of theological difference. Fuller Seminary in 1955 was too close to its partly fundamentalist origins for these sentiments to pass unchallenged. Conservatives on the faculty suggested that Carnell's sentiments smacked of theological compromise and blocked the publication of his address. (Only after Carnell's death did his former student, President David Hubbard of Fuller Seminary, have it published.)

The controversy over Carnell's inaugural address at Fuller was part of the background for the most controversial part of his much-discussed book, *The Case for Orthodox Theology* (1959). By the later

1950s, even though Carnell had not had the national impact for which he had hoped, he did have the satisfaction that mainline Protestant leaders were recognizing him as one of the most thoughtful evangelical spokesmen. He was honored to play this role when he was chosen by Westminster Press to write a book on evangelicalism to complement books on Protestant liberalism and neo-orthodoxy in a three-part series. While Carnell defended broadly Reformed orthodoxy, the most notable part of his book was his polemic against fundamentalism. Not only did he attack dispensationalist theology and fundamentalist anti-intellectualism, but he also singled out conservative Protestantism's most renowned scholar, J. Gresham Machen (1881–1937), for some of his strongest criticism. Carnell characterized Machen, the founder of Westminster Theological Seminary and the Orthodox Presbyterian Church, as promoting a "cultic mentality" which Carnell saw as one of the worst features of fundamentalism. Even though Carnell had resigned from the Fuller presidency at just about the same time that *The Case for Orthodoxy* appeared, the book brought widespread criticism from conservatives and fundamentalists to Fuller Theological Seminary and to its sponsor, Charles E. Fuller.

Carnell resigned the presidency largely because of deteriorating mental health. His condition was doubtless exacerbated by the immense pressures of the presidency while also continuing with his scholarship. In the subsequent years he suffered from bouts of severe depression and during the worst period in 1961–62 he was hospitalized for five weeks and then continued an extensive series of shock treatments or electroconvulsive therapy. Nonetheless, he continued his teaching and some writing, although as a teacher he was only a shadow of himself. He also maintained his role as an evangelical spokesperson on the national scene, continuing to write for the *Christian Century* and other journals articles that would be collected posthumously in *The Case for Biblical Christianity*, edited by Ronald H. Nash. Most notably he accepted, despite his illness, the great honor of being one of the "young theologians" chosen to dialogue with theologian Karl Barth on his much-heralded visit to the United States in 1962.

Before the most severe onset of his illness, Carnell had completed yet another apologetic work, *The Kingdom of Love and the Pride of Life* (1960). Once again he shifted his emphasis and tone. In dealing with his psychological difficulties he had been reading Freud and he incorporated insights from modern psychology into his work. As in much of his writing, he generalized from personal insight into the human condition. In this case he emphasized the universal need for love that Christianity offered as a counter to destructive pride. His only major publication after his illness was *The Burden of Søren Kierkegaard*, which drew on work he had done for his Boston University doctoral dissertation.

In May of 1967 Carnell was to be one of three keynote speakers at a Roman Catholic ecumenical conference in Oakland, California. On the day of the conference he was found dead in his hotel room from an apparent accidental overdose of sleeping pills.

Carnell's spectacular successes, his even higher ambitions, his disappointments, and his profound inner struggles make him one of the most intriguing figures in this history of American evangelicalism. His writings often combine incisive logic with introspection. In them one can both find the products of one of the finest minds of the time and get glimpses of what might be characterized as "the burden of Edward J. Carnell."

—George M. Marsden
2007

PREFACE

Not long ago we smiled rather skeptically when men of science prophesied that within our own generation every home would be a theater. Such fantasies appeared no more likely of fulfillment then than does a round-trip excursion to the moon today.

Our faithlessness was soon challenged, however! One evening, lo, we discovered ourselves milling in the midst of a wide-eyed crowd of people, watching for the first time the marvels of a receiving set equipped with its own animated screen. The picture which the new invention displayed was not technically perfect, to be sure; but there, proud in the Main Street appliance store, was concrete evidence that the early prophets of science voiced more truth than fiction. In all of its glistening, spanking newness was the marvelous electronic medium: *television*.

While much about this new medium remains hazy, one thing is certain: Television is here to stay. During a few short years of experiment, TV has absorbed, sufficient money from those having faith in its possibilities to emerge as one of the ten leading industries in the nation. Although fear and uncertainty may stalk the corridors of many post-war economies, those who control television are surcharged with enthusiasm. It is questionable whether there has ever been a time in the history of free enterprise when so many people have been willing to invest so freely in something which has been so consistent and greedy in its losses. Millions of profitless dollars are being invested every year by television speculators. And yet, unbelievably, this astronomical deficit is reckoned negligible when matched against the unlimited future of the medium. TV looms before television experts as did the automobile in the imagination of Henry Ford: The thing is too good to be a loser.

While an eager industry tools up the new giant, however, concerned parents, pastors, and educators cannot but wonder how this Gargantuan monster is going to affect the manners and morals of the nation. Those who believe in changeless truth, in eternal values, in fine art, in short, those who believe in God, view the growth of TV with a healthy caution. They understand clearly that TV's limitless possibilities for good are never unmixed with limitless possibilities for evil. Whatever is dynamic enough to emerge as a dictator over the minds of men for good, will also bear along with it the power to mold the minds of men for evil.

This volume is sort of an anticipatory balance sheet. It is an attempt—however inadequate—to sum up what appear at this point in history to be the major virtues and vices of television. All entries remain theoretical, of course, inasmuch as TV is too youthful and supple to lodge contained within ossified categories of finality. The volume (in military terms) is projected on the strength of a calculated risk. Since, however, the issues involved are grave and the time to meet them slight, courageous advance must be made even within the limitations of probabilities.

Mindful of this, the author writes in the mood of old Scrooge as described in Dickens' *A Christmas Carol*: "Men's courses will foreshadow certain ends, to which, if persevered in, they must lead. But if the courses be departed from, the ends will change." We do not presume to calculate what television *will* do to the manners and morals of men; we only seek to appraise some of the contributions (good and bad) which television *may* make. The policies of those who control the medium, together with the interaction of the televiewers themselves, must determine whether or not any of these potential contributions will ever be actualized.

The book is shaped like a sandwich: Concluding and introductory chapters are the bread, while the meat is formed of six units of discussion on the pro and con of video. In the order of presentation the good is examined before the threatened evil. This method is not only psychologically wise, but it is the course of ordinary prudence. No one advances human well-being by making capital out of unrighteousness.

In electing a standard by which TV is to be judged, the author has chosen that world view upon which western culture rests: *Christianity*. Reasons to support the wisdom of this decision will appear in the course of the following chapters.

Each generation must soberly measure the vitality of those powers which emerge in history to capture the imagination and allegiance of men, for the security of one generation often turns on the vigilance of the preceding. No culture is ever so secure that it need not periodically re-examine the vitality of its own main beams and crossbeams.

Interpreting, directing, and understanding television is the responsibility of *this* generation. Whether it will strengthen or corrode the foundations of our culture depends entirely upon what we determine to do with it.

The author wishes to acknowledge an indebtedness to his colleagues, Dr. Carl F. H. Henry and Dr. Gleason Archer, Jr., and to the seminary physician, Dr. Earle Newhart, for their critical reading of an earlier draft of the volume. For the contents of the final manuscript, however, the author alone assumes full responsibility.

The Scripture quotations in this publication are from the Revised Standard Version of the New Testament, copyrighted 1946 by the International Council of Religious Education and are used by permission.

Fuller Theological Seminary
Pasadena, California   E. J. C.

TABLE OF CONTENTS

Preface 5

I. The Collision of the Two Cities 13

II. The Magical World of Enchantment 26

III. *Savior Faire*, Please 47

IV. Read the Label and See for Yourselves 70

V. Love Not Sleep Lest You Come to Poverty 108

VI. The World, the Flesh, and Video 137

VII. Delicate Roots Require Tender Care 165

VIII. The Vertical Reference 192

TELEVISION

I

The Collision of the Two Cities

"Professor," cried a young freshman, overtaking his philosophy instructor on the campus of a large university.

"Yes, son?" came the swift answer. The sage was anxious to move on to his research.

"It may sound strange, sir," said the freshman, "but I was concerned to know whether there is any word which may be applied to everything in nature. Everything has 'being,' I know. But will any other term cover all the things on this earth?"

"Mixture," said the professor.

"*Mixture?*" responded the student. "I don't understand."

Without another word the professor reached out and pulled down one of the low branches of the spreading dogwood tree under which they stood. Close examination of the flowers revealed to the surprised freshman the fact of mixture. The pink blossoms had dapples of white in them and the white had flecks of pink. Furthermore, both pink and white flowers were growing on the same tree. Here was mixture.

It was not long before the lad began to see the point.

"There is nothing perfectly pure in nature, son. Learn this truth early in life and you will spare yourself much disappointment and grief. All things in nature are streaked with mixture. If you seek perfection, look to the timeless archetypes in God."

With this, the conversation ended. The professor plucked a dogwood blossom for his lapel and springily made his way over to the rare book library.

1. *The universality of mixture.* The boy did not have to wait until he was a college senior to detect the profundity in the sage's insight. Fellow freshmen, who otherwise professed honesty and kindness, were noticed cheating on important final examinations. Here was mixture in the lives of men. Even the professors were irregular in the skill of their presentation. One day they moved the class with their dynamic insights into truth, while the very next they were champions of perfect boredom. But above all, the lad sensed a mixture mode in his own living. Both his thoughts and his actions were tainted with the conflicting tendencies of good and bad.

Soon he discovered that the natural world, likewise, fell under the category of mixture. The leaf on the Norway Maple tree was not perfectly smooth on its surface as he had thought. Microscopic examination showed a roughness and irregularity. The lad's pocket no longer held perfect acorns, for the most exacting circle in nature is marked by deflection. There are no perfect figures in nature, no absolute colors, no consistent textures.

It took only a slight deduction to conclude, further, that if men's inward motives are mixed, the works of their hands must be imperfect, too. Is the servant greater than the master? Every piece of art, every cultural token, every invention—however enrapturing when first appraised—reveals, when minutely scrutinized, some areas of defection mottled in with the perfection. The absolute is known by the artist only as an ideal to be striven unto, never as a reality achieved. The most splendid canvas, the most exquisite marble work, the finest jeweled piece is chipped or flawed somewhere, regardless how matchless the whole may appear on the surface to be. Every piece of technology is miscalculated at some point. Every volume published is scarred with typographical errors. Mixture, like the poor, is with us always.

2. *TV and mixture.* If the unmixed is, like the horizon, an absolute which recedes the more closely one draws near, one would err, not heeding the professor's sagacious insight, if he

believed that television, another work of fallible men, is an unmixed medium: wholly good or wholly bad. Because the hearts of those who control the medium are streaked and uneven, the same mixture is bound to carry over into the finished instrument. Perfection, like water, cannot rise above its source. Video is bound to be no purer in its good or bad offerings than the inconsistent moral natures of those who dictate station policies.

Television is compounded with the freedom of man. Freedom is that soaring power in man, that scheme of imagination through the power of which one can overtake both himself and his historical limitations. There is no locus in history, no personal decision, which cannot be overreached by a free man's imagination to be converted into wider, creative potentialities. A society which pronounces a finality on itself is an organism large with the elements of its own destruction. While it comfortably abandons further progress in the name of a premature finality, enemy nations are energetically making plans for world domination. History has a fluid front; it is always in change. Each generation is qualified to master and exploit the insights and triumphs of the preceding.

This ability of freedom, however, can be either a blessing or a bane, depending upon the moral nature of the one directing it. A free man has power to create, and he has power to destroy. Skilled creation represents the outside possibilities of man's *positive* freedom, as illustrated in the creative work of libraries, hospitals, cultures, art, science, worship. Vitriolic destruction is the *negative* threat of freedom, the power to kill, maim, dynamite, torture, corrode. In a free man's hand a shimmering blade can slice bread to nourish the infant, or it can be plunged into the little one's heart. A free spirit may forgive or extort, heal or poison, love or hate, obey or rebel. Television lies within the pincers of these alternatives: It can propagate the good or it can herald the bad. All turns on what a free man elects to do.

3. *The problem of television standards.* The moment one speaks of a divided value in television, however, it is necessary that he be cautious in his definition of good and bad. How may one either charge video with threats of evil or praise it for its powers for good, until he has an unambiguous understanding of what make up the good and bad, the worthy and unworthy? The carpenter has a yardstick to measure a board. The musician evaluates the note by the criterion of perfect pitch. But by what standard may we judge the worth and mixture of TV?

We may profitably turn to the wisdom of the venerable Plato for a partial solution to our dilemma. In the minds of the Greeks a work is good when it measures up to the pattern or purpose for which it was made or intended. The bridge is good when it functions well within the definition of such a span. A harp is good when it emits harmonies. A ship is good when it performs serviceably as a self-propelled vehicle of water transportation.

If this is all that is involved in the problem of standards, one may quickly conclude that television is not only good, but excellent. If, in its case, the good is simply the electronic communication of ideas, TV is very good indeed. In the long and glorious history of scientific labor no more powerful, no more efficient, means to relay ideas to the masses of the people has been devised. Because it synthesizes the agility and economy of radio with the mobility, popularity, accessibility, vividness, and straightforwardness of the films, it is exceedingly difficult even to conceive of a way in which a more excellent communication device might be assembled. All who have intimately experienced the magnetic power of this new-born, parlor giant sense that it passes all its technology tests *summa cum laude.*

4. *Beyond the Greeks.* The alerted reader, however, can detect by now that this Platonic digression is really beside the point. The crucial, core-problem of television is neither the instrument itself nor its technological might, but rather the hands and hearts of him who owns and controls video. The crucial problem, therefore, is one of *ethics.* Ethics is the science

of conduct. It is that branch of learning which tells a man what *ought* to be and how he *ought* to conduct himself. The Ten Commandments, for example, are rules of ethics. In no meaningful sense, thus, can we say that the TV set itself is our problem. Our problem is, was, and shall be, *man*. If man can control himself, television will take care of itself.

But what is man's right? What is the wrong? And how can those who own and control television learn whether they are acting worthily or unworthily?

These are excellent questions, and they point to the complexity of this business of right living. Perhaps, however, one might best move into the area of answer along the course of negation. If pearls appear the more brilliant when set against the backdrop of soft, black velvet, Christianity, the fountainhead of western culture, will be enhanced if understood against competing alternatives.

The first alternative is *skepticism*. If a television magnate laughs at the thought that there are changeless, ethical rules which ought to govern his station policies, declaring, rather, that each man is a law unto himself, such a man is a skeptic. A skeptic denies that there are universal rules of right and wrong which all men must obey. A skeptic is a law unto himself. A skeptic only smiles at the suggestion that a man *ought* to do this or that. The good is just what happens to appeal to his own taste at a given time, just as he believes the good of the nation to be what happens to satisfy it.

Intuition tells us that skepticism is not true. When the judge sentences a man to die in the electric chair, he cannot be acting on motives so trivial as the skeptic's position would seem to require. It is not simply a matter of arbitrary expediency that people be put to death. Death is a penalty for law, and law is higher than personal likes or dislikes. The early effort of television executives to write a moral code for the medium is indicative of the uneasy conscience of those who rule the industry. There is a law higher than the individual, and those who destroy the lives of men are guilty whether they use a gun, tear gas, or television.

A higher position than skepticism is *dictatorship*. Stalin is a dictator. What he decides upon is good, and what he condemns is bad. In television, perhaps, it may be the president of the company or the most powerful advertiser who is thought to have the right to settle problems of ethics in the industry. He becomes a TV dictator.

Dictatorship is a pathetic alternative, for dictators themselves may be either good or bad, sinful or righteous. There are good sovereigns and there are wicked despots. So, may not the president of a TV industry himself be a proud, egotistic, domineering person who officiously rules a corporation with a wicked heart? "As a roaring lion, and a ranging bear; so is a wicked ruler over the poor people." (Proverbs 28:15) Since a dictator may be put under criticism, it follows that he is subject to a law higher than himself.

A superficially convincing, but equally inadequate, solution is the belief that the *will of an entire people* determines what shall constitute the rules of right and wrong. In this instance the television industry need only appeal to the public mind for standards. If public opinion votes that a program is helpful, then that program is good; while if a reverse decision is handed down, the program is bad. It is but a simple matter of the way people decide to vote. Let us assume, for example, that certain television programs begin taking the name of God in vain. The people then vote on the matter. If they vote that no harm is being done, then swearing over a public medium becomes a good thing. If they vote that ill is being stimulated, then the swearing is a bad thing. It all turns on the vote of the people.

This position is unsatisfactory, likewise. Nations as well as individuals can be good or bad, worthy or unworthy. It is the irresponsible, emotional mind, not the thoughtful citizen, who cries, "My country, right or wrong." If an *individual* may be right or wrong, so may the state. One does not change a bad to a good, a wrong to a right, simply by increasing the size of the unit involved. Extreme nationalism is just another form of skepticism.

Those who control television are responsible to all the people in the world, not to a limited group in any single country. If television is used to stir up a nationalistic spirit which leads to war, those who control it are wicked. If it is used to arouse race hatred, once again blame lies at the doors of those in power. Video executives, like all men, are subject to a rule which stands over all the nations. Without an eternal standard to judge the changing relativities of national decision, the world will be turned into an arena of gang and hoodlum warfare. In an atomic age, TV men must realize that either they and all men are subject to changeless laws of right and wrong, decency and indecency, or that might makes right. If the second alternative is true, that nation which happens to accumulate the greatest number of atomic bombs becomes the most righteous. But the first thing that such a "righteous" nation may decide on is to hang by the neck all who own and control television.

Western culture has succeeded only on the strength of the insight that the will and mind of God, as revealed in the Ten Commandments and in Jesus Christ, can successfully standardize the ethical judgments of men. Christianity—whatever else it may be—is at least a view of life and death which insists that it makes a real difference in affairs how a man conducts himself. Christianity says that there is a God who will judge all men for deeds done in the flesh. It preaches that God has put His laws deep in the heart of all men and will require from them an account of their stewardship. Right and wrong, justice and injustice, thus, are ethical laws written deep in the fabric of the universe. Whereas the laws of physics may change with deeper insights into the nature of the universe, the basic ethical laws of kindness, justice, purity, and holiness will never change. They define man in his changeless nature, themselves being unconditioned by the changing moods of history.

A television age forms no exception to the rule that all men are bound by the law of God and that right and wrong, decency and indecency, are standards which proceed from the eternal will of God and are not formulated by the arbitrary decisions of men in history.

Television will be used effectively by free men only if it is kept in harmony with the revealed will of God Almighty. In Christ a standard of forgiving love is found which is binding on all generations. In Christ the nature of man is so exhausted, that anything less than His mind entails a retreat to skepticism. If television men use the new medium to increase hatred, lust, or selfishness, therefore, they, by colliding with the will of God for man, become wicked and unworthy men. But if television is used to increase love, chastity, and altruism, then it is a means by which its executives may hear God's "Well done."

The United States of America, which stamps on certain coins, "In God we trust," pledges its allegiance, not to a dictator, not to the abstract will of the people, but to God. When the president is inaugurated, hence, he bows to kiss the Bible as a token to the world that the rulers which be are ordained of God and that there is no power given to man except that which comes from God. Either the television industry stamps at the top of its ideals, "In God we trust," or it will discover its powers discontinuously related to those spiritual vitalities and harmonies for the preservation of which the patriots and minute men of old fought and died on the fields of battle.

There is no satisfying alternative: Either God is the captain of the television industry, or man is. If God is, then the American people can bow in prayer for thankfulness that this mighty force—equal to that of atomic power—has fallen into the hands of godly spirits. But if autonomous man is in sovereign control, then a day of mourning is in order. In the hands of men and women who care not for the objective law of God, TV may undermine those pillars upon which the nation's heritage in righteousness rests.

5. *The two citizens and the two cities.* Because God is personal and because some love and follow His law while others do not, society is divided into what Augustine called "the two cities." Those who love both God and His law are *children of light*. They have found the highest rule, the sublimest order. "Oh how I love thy law! It is my meditation all the day." (Psalm 119:97) The children of light are citizens of the city of God. They confess that they are "strangers and exiles on the earth." (Hebrews 11:13)

Over against these stand the *children of darkness*, those who are a law unto themselves, who love neither God nor His law. "You are of your father the devil, and your will is to do your father's desires." (John 8:44) The children of darkness are citizens of this world. They confess only that this world is their home. They refuse to come to the light, lest the intentions of their hearts be exposed.

All of society is comprised of the citizenry of these two cities. This is the profoundest reason why television will inevitably remain a mixed offering. Children of light are bound to labor side by side with the children of darkness in the production, direction, and maintenance of the new medium. If the fountain waters are divided against themselves, dare one expect the flow to be pure? From mixture only mixture can come. It would be unrealistic to believe that TV will be either all good or all bad. The children of light will remain the salt of television, preserving TV from corruption and spoilage; while the children of darkness will tend to be a gravitation force in video for its secularization. As long as the collision of the two cities continues within society, each group will incline to complement the other, cancelling out a consistent turn in television for either pure righteousness or pure unrighteousness. Both those who throw a halo over television, thinking that nothing but good will come from it, on the one hand, and those who decry it as an unalloyed voice of unrighteousness, on the other, fail to recognize the ubiquity and inevitability of the category of mixture in nature and society.

There is yet another reason, however, why television is certain to be a mixed force in society. Since neither the children of light nor the children of darkness are consistent in their professions, a new and more complex mixture emerges. The godly, who have confessed their cordial relation to God Almighty, for example, frequently discover in their daily lives that they are unable to match in practice what they profess in faith. "For I do not do the good I want, but the evil I do not want is what I do." (Romans 7:19) It is the honest admission of all the righteous that the law of God requires a duty of selfless love to God and to one's neighbor which is never actually fulfilled in daily living. In the holiest of men there lurks those demonic vitalities of pride and egotism which are the accelerating powers in all actual sin.

The same inconsistency is displayed among atheistic, skeptic children of darkness. While professing no fear of God or of His holy law, most of the citizens of this world conduct themselves in a quasi-righteous way. The man of the street, he who never darkens the church door, is surprisingly upright in his ways. He responds to mercy cries; he never steals; he pays his taxes on time; and he would prefer his own death to the murder of another.

Somewhere in this maze of complexity of motives, intentions, and deeds, television lies. Technological efficency is a neutral powder keg: It can move the world for God, or it can blow civilization apart. These termini define the outside limits of TV's promises and threats.

However, only unrealism and fanaticism would council the belief that either of these possibilities will ever be realized in history, for the inconsistencies of both the children of light and the children of darkness will guarantee that television will be neither purely good nor purely bad.

The danger of the children of this world is to look at television with rose-colored glasses, seeing and appreciating only the good in the medium, but being completely blinded to its threats. The danger of the children of the city of God is to look at television through the glasses of a heavenly perfectionism, noticing only the defects and blemishes of the medium by applying too pure and holy a criterion to an earthly mixture. If sanity and realism are to be maintained, both the righteous and the unrighteous must awaken to the mixed state of all historical contingencies. Every dogwood blossom is mottled with mixture. The children of darkness must learn that earth is not heaven, while the children of light must learn that the earth, while not heaven, is not hell. The earth is a mixed affair. Until God's appointed end, the collision of the two cities will continue.

6. *The mid-twentieth century watchword: vigilance.* While it is true that history will never harbor either pure evil or pure good among the sons of men, the shifting front of a moving culture seems at times to expose a lower kindling point for the fires of sin and unrighteousness than at others. Modern man appears to be passing over one of these powder-keg surfaces in history today. Unusual vigilance must be kept on all fronts of our culture, therefore, lest the children of darkness, encour-

aged by token successes, become intoxicated with the dream of world domination.

Nothing is more characteristic of this "aspirin age" than that fear and unrest which characterizes a people whose technological insight has outrun their moral strength. The pleasure of man recently was the comfortable hope of an impending utopia. Today his cry is survival. The fear of war is universal. Uncertainty is on every hand. And what may account for this new trend toward pessimism and fear? The answer is not exhausted in the observation that wicked men are on the increase, although surely such an observation may not easily be gainsaid. The profound answer, rather, is that the children of this world are being outfitted by science with those instruments of communication and destruction which lend an air of efficiency to their mad schemes of world conquest and domination. It is a secure fact in the science of criminology that possession of mechanical and technological instruments inflates the pride, and blinds the moral sense, of the aggressor in direct proportion to the power of the weapons. A coward would not injure even a child in his own strength; but when fortified by a brandished machine gun he boldly pilfers the contents of a bank during rush hours. The difference between the criminal dictator, who threatens to plunge civilization into the darkness of World War III, and the criminal behind prison bars, who cannot harm social life, is simply a wicked freedom within the fortification of technological efficiency. The dictator is both proud and dangerous because he holds the guns, tanks, and planes required to surround his cowardness. The other criminal's potentialities for aggression are contained within him. If, however, the incarcerated thief ever enjoyed the technological security of the mad dictator, he would surely terrorize the world with his dreams of dominion and plunder. No strategy of the Comintern was ever more bloody in its intent, or planned with greater meticulosity, than the lethal programs conjured up by felons serving life sentences in federal prisons.

In the light of the desperation of the modern scene, the mixture of television protrudes in bold relief. Video may be likened to a powerful, new medicine: If taken in proper doses, it will perform miracles for man; but if the directions given on the bottle are not carefully followed, it may bring instant death. Television can become a medium for the endless increase of human happiness and security. This is our hope. But it may fall into the hands of those who will use it as a further means to exploit sinful potentialities in man. This is our fear. Between the tensions of fear and hope we must tack, relaxing neither alternative at any point.

Inasmuch as TV has placed the warfare of the two cities in the parlor, to be a direct influence on all, the time needed to mold the minds of the masses of men has been made frightfully short. Whereas it formerly required years to propagandize a nation, the task may now be accomplished almost overnight. America's anxiety over the atom bomb and biological warfare, violent and lethal as such powers may be, must not blind it to the Trojan-horse threats of television. Men who are free are free both to create and to destroy. Thus, with every hopeful promise of TV there rides, like poliomyelitis germs on the dawning of a mid-summer's day, the crippling virus of evil.

Lest a premature pessimism overtake us, however, so that we lose the gains already made through our insight into the mixed character of nature, let us quickly counterbalance early fears with a realistic study of TV's hopes. Only when we have had the endless good of video charted before us will we be in that sympathetic and patient frame of mind required to evaluate the threats of TV to our culture. Let us turn at once to a positive study of video.

II

The Magical World of Enchantment

When the Ringling Brothers and Barnum and Bailey Circus made its annual visit to Madison Square Garden in the spring of 1948, a new feature was added to the "Greatest Show on Earth:" The colossal enterprise was televised. A spectacular applause from big-eyed televiewers resulted. Thousands of people up and down the east coast, from every walk of life, perched in front of their TV sets, electrified by the magnificence and weight of the prodigious performance. The Hooper Rating, gleaned from a quick tallying of program response, pronounced the circus telecast a smashing success. A battery of alert telephoto-lensed video cameras, strategically mounted throughout the show place, relayed to the eager audience a range of details from the tiger's bored yawn to the apprehensiveness in the eye of the leaping high-wire performer. Five three-hour telecasts of the Ringling Brothers and Barnum and Bailey circus convinced even the most skeptical that the world had seriously entered the television era. TV was no longer a fledgling. As one news reporter described it, television brought everything to the home but color and the circus smell.

1. *The laughing animal.* When one turns to explain why it is that the circus met such an anxious, chuckling audience over television, he must postulate that the nature of man is such that it craves fun and laughter. Keeping man laughing and relaxed is one of the responsibilities of video. And there is

very little doubt but what the medium will competently rise to the occasion.

Since the beginning of recorded history, man has characterized himself as the animal who loves to be entertained. Ancient Roman emperors perpetuated their pedestal of favor by supplying the masses with generous portions of bread and circus. Chariot races, gladiator events, and animal fights, while not the most wholesome form of entertainment, were enthusiastically received by the docile masses. In medieval times wandering minstrels, jugglers, buffoons, jesters, and puppet artists accrued both a lucrative income and rich personal satisfaction from placating man's urge to be entertained. In modern times a maze of agencies vie together to scoop off some of the billions of dollars spent each year by lovers of circus. These agencies are underwritten by the common faith that human beings fare better in Winston Churchill's world of "blood and sweat and tears" if they relax now and then to dream and smile in the magical world of enchantment.

Homo sapiens, being a very complex and, at times, exasperating creature, has been defined in many different ways. Some thinkers are so bold as to label man "a featherless biped," while others, such as the pessimistic Nietzsche, feel satisfied with the belief that man is "an animal which blushes." Medieval scholastics, faithful to the Aristotelian tradition, define man as "a rational animal." Modern Protestants believe him to be "a sentient creature qualified to worship God." Although our intention is not to add further complexity to an already overworked subject, let us, for the sake of the point being made in this chapter, define man as "an animal who laughs." Language has a certain arbitrariousness to it. As head lettuce in salads, it may be used in endless combinations.

A wise man once remarked that an expert thinker can be detected by his ability to understand mathematics and his skill in catching on to profound jokes. Now, while all understand why the one who can perceive mathematical abstractions is a profound thinker, few remember that it also takes a keen mind to see through good jokes. The relations in mathematics are purely *congruous,* as when two times two equals four. When a person understands what is meant by the symbol "one," he can then immediately detect the truth and coherence of the mathematical relationship. Humor, however, is created out of *incongruent* relations, as when the young couple were asked how far it was between Dan and Beersheba, responded with surprise that they thought Dan and Beersheba were husband and wife like Sodom and Gomorrah. Seeing and understanding humorous relations is as fine an art as mathematics any day. And, furthermore, it is much more fun.

Very few children of light think highly enough of themselves at this point, however. They sometimes have a feeling that laughter is but a frivolous appendage to man's serious nature, and that in the act of laughing man leaves the real kingdom of *Homo sapiens* for that instability of the animal kingdom where emotions, not the intellect, rule. Nothing could be further from the truth. Man is at his best, not his worst, when he is smiling. Out of the entire animal kingdom only man can laugh. The horse at times looks like it is laughing, but it really is not; for laughter presupposes the freedom of the rational mind to perceive and appreciate incongruity. The baboon in the zoo is not laughing when it watches the puzzled faces peering at it through the bars. Neither the horse nor the baboon possesses that free exercise of reason and imagination which must be presupposed if abstract symbolic relations are to be recognized. There is not a horse in the world which would give a cup of oats for a whole company of entertainers. But man is different —nay, vastly different. He will sell the shoes off his feet for the privilege of hearing and telling jokes.

Unless, therefore, this capacity for laughter is understood, man cannot be appreciated in the full height of his freedom. There is "a time to laugh . . . and a time to dance." (Ecclesiastes 3:4) Whoever severs the tie which binds man to the magical world of enchantment, therefore, robs human fullness of part of its glory.

One of the most serious challenges that television has to meet is that of keeping men entertained with wholesome programs. And there is little doubt but what this side of video's schedule will be well padded. Entertainers from every walk of life, some questionable, others commendable, have already set their foot lockers inside the TV studios. However, before one leaps to hasty conclusions about either the caliber or the worthwhileness of television's entertainment programs, he had best be cautious not to underestimate the responsibility of the new medium to keep man laughing. Man is a laughing animal, and unless he smiles now and then he will dry up inside and die.

2. *Laughter and inward morale.* If the task of keeping man at ease with himself and the world through entertainment is not important, why is it that in every war the nation supplies millions of dollars worth of gear to help singers, musicians, and comedians put across their programs to the boys and girls in uniform? The answer is easy. Through the introduction of some diversional pleasure into the sweaty routine of army life, the uniformed man finds inward relief from the tensions of the day. Relaxation is sort of an escape valve in the heart of man, releasing pent-up emotions and fears through fun and laughter. The "stage door canteen" was as important to every G. I. in World War II as tanks and bullets could ever be. Only that soldier who learned the art of relaxing now and then was qualified to bear up under the stress and strain of battle. The armed forces traveled light, indeed, but not so light that they had to leave behind their companies of entertainers. Battles are lost

when morale perishes. A soldier without an incentive to fight is a less effective soldier than the one who has gained inward integration. As sleep is to the body—refreshing, invigorating, and renewing—so laughter is to the spirit.

All men, in a very real sense of the term, are soldiers. Both the species of the battle and the field upon which it is fought may differ from that of the G. I., indeed, but both struggle in a conflict. Some labor in school, others in a steel foundry or coal mine, and still others battle icy winds on the high seas. While their warfare is carried on with brooms, nets, cranes, picks, and typewriters, instead of planes, flame throwers, and mortars they are still locked in conflict. The battle is against the proverbial "weary round of life." Many returning soldiers have found this battle even more taxing than that of martial combat. The business man boards the suburban commuter train hurriedly, endures a pressing day in the office, only to return at night, after being jostled and shoved in the subways, to begin the drudgery all over again. If, at the end of such a thankless routine, all this business man has to show for his labors is, as one has aptly put it, "a station wagon and an annuity policy," it does not presuppose a large measure of prophetic intelligence to conclude that there is something very, very futile about this whole affair of living. All who are caught in the maelstrom of the work-a-day world know intuitively that their own morale must be kept just as delicately balanced as that of the soldier in the field.

It is questionable whether television has any higher role to play than that of preventing the masses of the people from facing the weariness of the routine of life. The comedian is an ally of both clergyman and doctor when he elicits smiles from the discouraged coal miner who, black from the pits and pessimistic over the future economy of the coal market, ponders the worthwhileness of the whole effort to live. One need not be a child of light to appreciate the worth of this philanthropic role which TV is asked to play. It is only a question of common kindness that a cool glass of water be given to those who are thirsty. If the means are wholesome, one should praise the effort.

Through its almost unbelievable efficiency and economy, video is more than capable of entertaining the masses and keeping morale high. It can reach into the one-room apartment of the lonely secretary as she passes the hours of the evening, longing for companionship. It can stand beside the bed of the one who is imprisoned by physical infirmities, wafting him away by the Aladdin-Lamp magic of its cathode-ray tube. Hail to television!

To anticipate an objection which may here be raised by the children of light, however, a note of caution must be interjected. It is not being proposed, nor should it ever be, that *ultimate* satisfaction in the inward spirit of a man can ever be gained through earthly entertainment. Only God can give the whole man satisfaction. As Augustine has immortalized it, "Man was made unto God and he will not rest until he rests in God." Neither the soldier at the canteen nor the weary coal worker before television will discover either perfect or lasting satisfaction for his heart through entertainment. Entertainment is but *part* of the answer to man's predicament. The *real* answer is Jesus Christ.

Solomon, who made a test case out of the tensile strength of earthly pleasures, came to the conclusion that earthly pleasures, being temporal, can give no more than temporal satisfaction. The song will fade, the dance end, the money vanish. But the spirit of man, craving for more satisfaction, will remain. "Let us hear the conclusion of the whole matter: Fear God, and keep his commandments: for this is the whole duty of man." (Ecclesiastes 12:13)

But what *is* being proposed—and this the children of light ought to be first to appreciate—is that man is still a laughing animal whether his citizenry is of this world or of heaven. All men ought to laugh heartily now and then. Collective humanity—righteous and unrighteous alike—crave the pleasures of the picnic, wedding, songs with old friends, a walk in the park. The dichotomy of either serving or not serving God is not even in question here. The point is that whether one serves God or the devil, he still is a human being, and as a human being he needs the placating and soothing release of fun and relaxation.

TV's entertainment blessings might be set in full relief by an imaginary journey in the mind's eye to the side of a bedridden invalid. Day in and day out, year in and year out, the confined person must sit and watch the same four walls, hoping inwardly all the while that the palliation of death might overtake him and end the sustained discomfitures. What inward pessimism he faces as he realizes that he will never again see the out of doors! Who can measure his frustration in having memorized every square inch in the room, hoping each time over that some uncovered area might be found to take the mind off the spatial limitations of the confinement? The nights are black and endless, one being set off from the other only by a variety in degrees of sleeplessness. Even the Stoic merits of suicide are carelessly toyed with. Now, into this despondency cast the tonic of television. By its magic TV can transport the sick instantly to every part of the world for a ringside participation in the fullness of life. The very word "television," itself, being a hybrid of the Greek and Latin words for *end* and *seeing*, means, literally, "distant seeing." Video promises to be the eyes and ears of the world, bringing to low and high alike everything which can be put within the all-seeing lens of the TV cameras.

When understood in its full resources, television is an invention for the appearance of which all men ought to thank the Almighty. When one sees limp and weak fingers return to vitality as the dial of the new medium is slowly turned, he then is in a position to confess that he has been the fool in his haste to underestimate the assistance TV can give men caught in the "weary routine of life."

3. *Relaxation and the therapies.* In the fine art of therapy, television has already taken over where radio left off. The Indiana State Prison, for example, reports that television appreciably saves on the flow of sedatives needed to calm its mental cases. And Dr. George E. Carlin, of the Louden-Knickerbocker Hall in Amityville, New York, after performing one of the most fascinating experiments yet projected, discovered that television takes the patient's mind off himself and temporarily permits him to lead a normal life again.

Since the body and soul are intimately interrelated, it is not surprising to discover that when a man cultivates a harmony in his soul, he is usually at home with himself in his body. Laughter has always been recognized by medics as a vital means by which needed hormones in the body are stimulated to flow. The body digests food better when man is happy. Peptic ulcers, which are the direct result of an over-neurosis, represent one end result of the mind's tearing the body apart through fretting and worry. However great may be the errors of such movements as Christian Science and the Unity Viewpoint, these religions are surely correct in their insistence that a healthy body is encouraged by an integrated mind. The heart works far better when one is completely unaware that he has such a thing as a heart. Worry over its performance only increases the possibility of its poor performance.

If television did nothing more than just make men happier with themselves, its existence would immediately be justified. Without a healthy body, a man cannot be fully himself.

Mental unbalance, however, is far more complex, far more tragic in its fruitage, and infinitely more difficult to cure than distortions of the body. While it is a pity to watch the distorted and ill-managed movements of a person struggling under the deformities of a crippled body, it is pure grief to see a mentally deficient individual. A bad body is a cross, but a bad mind is living death. Mental derangements are so intangible, so illusive, so everlasting in their torment, that any therapy which can break through with the balm of healing ought to be recognized for good. What can be sadder than the sight of a handsome, promising college student who, after years of mental discipline in the pursuit of education, has his mind snap, only to spend the rest of his natural life behind bars in a state institution for the violently insane? What is more delicate than the mind? While it will stretch and give, returning to vitality under the most unbelievable strains of routine, there is a limit to its resilience. It is a fact of experience that unless the mind is given opportunities for renewal through relaxation, it may finally lose its self-control.

One of video's proudest triumphs is that it, like the radio before it, can assist in the relief of mental pressure on this side of the hospital door. It can pleasantly induce people to replace inordinate self-concern with altruistic thoughts about the world and others.

TV's therapy is a welcomed anesthesia in this now proverbial "aspirin age." In this mid-twentieth century upheaval, where on every hand hearts are failing for fear, men must either retain the fine custom of relaxation or reckon with the threats of a destroyed equilibrium in body and soul. Well-being is not an automatic blessing. It must be cultivated with the same skill and artistry as growing a delicate rose. Television will painlessly assist in the mechanics of its cultivation.

Because most nervous difficulties grow out of excessive self-concern, the best thing for man is to take his eyes off himself and begin understanding others. One has wisely remarked that if all men had an opportunity to tie their personal problems into a bundle and then toss their separate bundles into a pile formed of the crosses of others; and if each was then afforded an equal opportunity to return to the pile and remove any one bundle and call it his own, every man would immediately rush back for his own pack. The reason for this quick recovery of one's own cross in preference to that of another is that personal burdens seem much lighter when weighed alongside the difficulties of a neighbor.

The service of increasing contentment can be performed by an ideal use of television. If man can be taught to turn away from his own worries, such worries will seem easier to bear.

At this point the children of light must guard against another premature censure. While it is true that television, by giving man *some* comfort, might contribute to the blinding of man to the more *ultimate* satisfactions in Christ, the Christian can not for this reason support the indefensible attitude that the natural man should be kept in poverty and grief until he finally solves his problems in Christ. There is such a thing as the parable of the Good Samaritan in the Bible. Here the principle of binding up the wounds of those in sorrow, regardless of race, creed, or color, is taught. If the children of darkness are forbidden a partial relief to their discomfitures, they will only recoil all the more stubbornly from the offer of final relief in the Lord Jesus Christ. By being kind to a perverse and wicked generation, rather than lordly, censorious, or faultfinding, the Christian will win that respect from the non-Christian which must be cultivated before the latter will hear and heed the gospel message.

4. *Relaxation and the increase of P.Q.* While it may be a less spectacular contribution, judged outwardly, the ability of television to promote the increase of P. Q. (personality quotient) in the land through its entertaining facilities is nonetheless far from being an unimportant matter.

If the first problem of man is learning to get along with oneself, the second is learning to get along with others. This second connection is called the "social" relation. The Latin, *socius,* means "associate" or "ally." Social relations, therefore, are relations of companionship, friendship, fellowship. The importance of social intercourse may be understood and appreciated partially when we remember that prisons define solitary confinement as a punishment. While it may be true that men seek temporary solitude for religious retreats or meditation, as an unbroken diet no man is ever happy in complete isolation. He is a gregarious, clustering, fellowshiping creature. Life is fully entered into only when the joys of social sharing are understood. Man is completely man only whenever he loves, shares, and fellowships. There is very little incentive for living when one has no one to live for. Daily experience teaches that lesson well.

Each individual is a well of social potentialities. Hidden in the recesses of his heart are powers of love, sacrifice, appreciation, and sympathy. But the warmth of these powers remain hidden, like sunbeams behind an early cloud, until they are drawn out by personality development. Personality may be defined as the outward expression of one's inward person. Nice personalities are those which exhibit love, sympathy, and the other social graces, while bad personalities show selfishness, a grumbling spirit, complaint. The world follows a pleasant personality, shunning all who display the grating characteristics of rancor, criticism, malignity, and resentment.

Because personality is such an asset in successful living, one can rejoice at the thought of video's battle against self-centeredness and self-complaceny in individuals. A pleasant personality is oil on turbulent waters, soothing and calming what might otherwise remain rough and unsettled. When loving relationships displace censorious and bickering attitudes, the home is made livable, the schoolroom harmonious, the office efficient, and the church unified. The man with a dynamic personality will locate employment for himself sooner, thus converting spiritual resources into material gain. A man with a delightful and invigorating personality never wants for friends, influence, power, prestige. Others turn to him for guidance and leadership, because they know that he who can pleasantly influence others is a man who has caught the meaning and value of social vitalities.

One quick way to release sweet, inward virtues is to smile. As is well known, "Laugh and the world laughs with you; weep and you weep alone." When a person smiles, he testifies that he enjoys inward harmony. One cannot laugh until he has taken his eyes critically off his own problems as an end in themselves and sees himself and his problems in the light of other issues. Only when our horizons are enlarged, can we laugh heartily. People love those who smile. A man who is free and easy in his own soul finds it easy to become concerned with the security and interest of others. It is the nervous, fretting individual who crucifies his P. Q. on the altar of selfish pursuits. Fretting and worrying corrodes and rusts the sweet vitalities of the spirit of man. Laughter breaks up the tension in the soul. It releases hidden, inward vitalities. The mood of joviality which prevails at the banquet table, one in which delightful harmonies between people are encouraged, proves conclusively that life is much richer when the mind is at ease.

Men who laugh together can also pray together. When the smile relieves pressure between personalities, a token proof of the union of mutual interests has been deposited. In prayer, interests are made cosmic. In prayer, men seek the face of God.

If used properly, television can teach people to relax and, in turn, increase their ability to move successfully in social relations. A husband or a wife who, fearful of entertaining others because they lack the self-confidence needed to sustain a lively and interesting conversation through the evening, will find television rising to the occasion by becoming a third party in the living room about which interest may turn. TV will strengthen personality contacts. Those who possess television sets are never in want of visiting friends. When it comes completely into its own, video will bring great drama, opera, or documentaries into the home for all to see. It is facile to entertain when there is plenty to do or see. TV will supply the bill.

When people just sit and stare at one another, the surface of new tension and criticism grows. Nothing is more easily misunderstood than a stare. Television will take eyes off persons in the room and place them in a world context.

There are real dangers attending too devoted an attitude toward television, to be sure; but pointing out these pitfalls is presently beside the point. People who lean heavily on entertainment may, indeed, lose, rather than gain, in personality quotient by not engaging in personal, friendly relations with others. That is true. The fact of mixture is still on hand. Yet the positive observation is still valid, that, carefully used, TV can increase rather than decrease national P. Q.

It is no easy thing for the average person to plan and guide group games when entertaining others. Only the exceptionally skilled can handle organized competition. From now on, however, video volunteers to bear the brunt of uniting group interests. Whenever there is a lull, snap on the television set. The formula is magical.

One of the major blocks to the continued preservation of a good personality spirit is the dullness inside of one which grows whenever life situations, by repeating themselves in too frequent cycles, become stale and vapid to the participant. It is the psychological experience of all that "familiarity breeds contempt." Because of this principle, it is salutary for husband and wife to leave home now and then to eat with friends or dine at a restaurant; for the departure will not only refresh the soul, thus increasing the flow of pleasant personality hormones, but also it will stimulate an appreciation for the home left behind. One never really understands the full value of a thing until it is taken away from him. Television, while not solving the problem absolutely—since it itself may also become a vapid routine—will go far in cracking the stubbornness of that feeling of contempt in man with what he senses is a drab, routine way of life. TV's variety is so wide, that a turnover in interests is certain to be more frequent. All this is to the good for the increase of personality sweetness.

Television will be a travel bureau in the home. "Everybody needs a holiday," is a popular (and true) magazine slogan. Whereas few have the means needed to enjoy world cruises, almost every family can afford a small television set. Video will transport the individual across the Sahara sands or over the hump to China, and all for the cost of a few pennies of electricity. When a person cannot go on a vacation, pressure within him, aroused by a pessimistic reaction to the routine of life, may grind the will into despondency. But when the moment arrives for the vacation, and the whole family prepares for something new, personality quotients increase geometrically. The whole family is knit together with the cords of mutuality as the suitcases are packed in the trunk of the automobile for the week's stay in the mountains or by the rolling sea. Forgiveness and understanding electrically charge the air as hearts beat high with anticipation. Roommates in college, who earlier flew at each other with impatience, lovingly embrace as they turn from the routine of school demands for the Christmas vacation at home. Walls of pride and self-interest crumble when a change in activity replaces the drabness of a routine existence.

TV bids fair to be a major personality booster in our generation, a generation so beset with problems that it needs an extra dose of relaxation for the cooling of nerves. Under the subdued lights in the living room the TV program will release inward vitalities of cordiality and understanding. The neighbor you just cannot seem to be able to fellowship with, will become your best friend when the cathode-ray tube of TV mediates the collision of your personality interests. It will be easy to forget your neighbor's large nose or that a borrowed lawn mower has not yet been returned when Toscanini raises his deft hands to lead the NBC Symphony Orchestra in Tschaikovsky's "Romeo and Juliet Overture," or when a filmed documentary on China exposes the poverty and ignominy of that poor people. Try it!

Not unrelated to P. Q. is the fact that only when a person nourishes a vital courage in his soul can he struggle for what he believes is the right. Every seminarian, for example, recalls the painful routine through which he passes in preparation for the gospel ministry. While tensions mounted high during the day, it was learned that if a break from the Greek and the Hebrew was made by the exchange of humor at the dinner table, a rousing song fest in the student commons, or a challenging round of ping-pong in the basement, courage was renewed to return to the study of the theological disciplines. This principle is true for all of living. A man will work much better in the morning if he has had a change from his routine at night. TV—which will probably remain an evening medium—will greatly increase courage through a break in routine.

5. *A danger in righteous reticence.* The children of this world need no encouragement to take from television all that it may offer by way of the increase of pleasure and fun in life. Because they have hope in neither Jesus Christ nor the good things to come, the children of darkness have made this earth their home. And since the earth is all they have, they mean to make the best of it. So, one result of the loss of heaven is that a compensation is attempted. Having no hope in things to come, the children of this world do their best to make a little heaven out of this world. Just as a blind man will train his fingers and ears to great sensitivity to compensate for the loss of eyesight, so the children of darkness, having lost the light of God, try to compensate by making full citizenship of themselves in this world. For this reason the children of this world have been quick to seize and utilize television to the full. No word of encouragement need be given to them!

A danger of the children of light, however, is that, having set their hope in things to come and having tasted the delights of salvation in Christ, they may be tempted to fall into the peril of under-evaluating the temporal blessings which God bestows on men. Faith in eternal things may be permitted to eclipse the subordinate values of this earth.

When He gave the instructive parable of the Unjust Steward, our Lord called to the attention of the children of light a danger to which they may become prey. One of the points to the parable is that those who fear God may, at times, be less skillful in the handling of earthly matters than the one who has never had his understanding opened to the eternal truths of the gospel. In matters of temporal efficiency, therefore, sometimes "the sons of this world are wiser in their own generation than the sons of light." (Luke 16:8) The conclusion itself is not startling, since it only stands to reason that those who spend all of their time and energy mastering temporal matters will become more dexterous in earthly assignments than those who live out their threescore years and ten in sober preparation for heaven. A philosopher (by way of simple illustration) may be quite content to spend the greatest share of his life meditating on cosmic problems, but he is foolish if he believes that at the end of such an expenditure of energy he is as competent in fixing pipes or repairing roofs as the rank and file among men who labor in these trades. Because the philosopher has left little or no time for such pursuits, he must learn to delegate them to those who have mastered them.

The children of light must not be perfectionists in their interpretation of life. History remains a mixed affair. The man who has been redeemed in Christ is still very much a feeble creature of dust. Nothing could be further from the truth than the conclusion that, since one has become a new creature in Christ, he no longer is in need of those temporal satisfactions of the body and spirit which assure an increase in happiness. A Christian coal miner or ditch digger is neither an angel nor half an angel. He is a human being who, having been redeemed from his sins, laughs, weeps, and sings. Contact with eternal values does not for the moment cancel out pleasure in the temporal. The outward life of the child of light is basically the same as that of the child of darkness. Both shop for food in the same store, and both return home weary at night to rest from the day's toil. Both wear clothing from the same flock of sheep, and both share the same booth when voting. Spiritual satisfaction from eating the flesh of Christ and drinking His blood does not destroy one's appetite for those cravings of the flesh which are satisfied in time and space. TV is no exception!

The Magical World of Enchantment

The children of light must tack on the door of their heart the eternal truth: "The earth is the Lord's, and the fulness thereof." (Psalm 24:1) If the children of God do not exploit this world for the glory of God, thus fulfilling the command of God to "subdue nature," they will unwittingly become less wise in their generation than the children of darkness who, sensing no satisfaction in God, yet make a conscientious effort to tap the earth for its fullness. If the children of this world ever sense that one of the conditions which they must meet in coming to Christ for redemption is abandoning all wholesome pleasures on earth, then they, temporarily wiser than the children of light, will cry with men of old: "If this be grace, give me nature!" God has put sufficient common sense in all men to teach them that part of man's nature lies unaccented when earthly pleasures are removed. Pleasure and relaxation are as natural to man as eating and breathing. The baby does not have to be taught to gurgle and coo. God gave the little one a human nature, and that nature is expressing itself in this manner. In fact, life without humor and fun is like a picnic without refreshments: a decidedly unsatisfying arrangement.

While Christ used great reserve and prudence in the course of His earthly ministry, He was yet quite at home with those who took pleasure seriously in life. He is called a "friend" of publicans and sinners in the Bible. His first miracle was turning water into wine at the wedding ceremony in Cana of Galilee. Knowing that there is nothing unclean which is harmoniously related to the perfect will of the Father, from Whom all things come, Christ drank freely of the world's fullness. Christians are bidden to *follow,* not try to surpass, their Lord.

The profoundest observation at this point is that the children of light may at times be more in need of wholesome earthly pleasures than the children of darkness who live night and day for this world. Christians are tense most of the time.

They are inwardly broken up over the sinfulness of the world. Like Paul the Apostle, they frequently weep for the lost condition of the world. The glacier-like progress of the gospel's spread causes increased concern in the Christian's spirit. Like his Lord, the Christian looks with great pity upon the multitudes who, being as sheep without a shepherd, move headlong into destruction on the broad road. One natural result of this unabated inward concern for the world's condition is that the child of light gravitates in the direction of a more conservative and sober philosophy of temporal existence than does the child of this world who fears no judgment to come. If tension is permitted to mount, the end of a good start in religion may be a complete nervous breakdown. The September, 1949 shooting of over a dozen persons in Camden, New Jersey, for example, an orgy in blood having no equal in the past records of the nation, was perpetrated by a religious, former army man who went on the maniacal rampage. He was known by his neighbors as the "Bible bug." Friends testified at his inquest that he often walked the streets, carrying a Bible under his arm. The boy's name is Howard Unruh. After his awful slaughter, Unruh went back to his room, where an open Bible lay on the table at Matthew, chapter twenty-four. Tragic though this case is, it is surely a warning to all the children of light that a good start with Christ may end in mental derangement if the mind is not given a chance to relax. Suppose that a mother pines away for her wayward son, watching him descend rung by rung down the ladder of decency into destruction, she may soon begin wearing herself away through the chronic tension. Unless she turns to other interests and allows her self-control to be regained, the sin of her son may only become an occasion for the greater sin of a broken mind.

The children of light must not fall prey to the fallacy of thinking that weeping over the sins of Jerusalem and attending weddings are incompatible activities. Whatever is of faith—including a wholesome interaction with television—is to be received with thanksgiving.

The rule of Christian living is as follows: "Whether you eat or drink, or whatever you do, do all to the glory of God." (I Corinthians 10:31) A healthy-minded Christian will evaluate television as part of the mixed order of the world's light and darkness, being careful to remove the good from the new medium, using it to the glory of God, while rejecting the unclean.

Nothing is clearer than the fact that God did not intend the world to be a bed of nettles for man. It is sin, and sin alone, which has entered a good universe to distort and corrupt its perfection. The thorns and thistles came as a result of God's pronouncements against sin and sinners. The Lord ordained harmony for man. Sin disturbed it. Yet, the pleasures of this world are still abundant and God-sanctioned. What would existence be like without joy? Without the pleasures of love, friendship, rest? The Lord has not decreed that man's way should be one of grief and travail. A television age forms no exception.

Should the children of light spurn the positive and wholesome in television in the name of a fidelity to eternal values, they will only exhibit their ingratitude for what God has done. Love never overlooks blessing. Suppose, for example, that a mother made a decade of heavy sacrifice so that her son might be provided with nice things for his schooling. And then suppose, further, that after having deprived herself of daily necessities in order that he might have shoes and a schoolbag, the son, out of a pretension of love to the mother, walks to school without shoes, borrows school supplies, and even leaves home out of a fear that he is a burden to his mother; would not this deliberate rejection of blessings reflect a decrease, not an increase, of love? In like manner, dare a Christian put his hand over his heart and say that he is glorifying and honoring His master when he turns aside from those tokens of esteem and love which the Father pours out?

The New Testament teaches that Christians are under a serious stewardship. They are to view their responsibility after the analogy of picking fruit from a tall tree. The children of light are to pick all of the fruit, for it all belongs to their Father. If they leave any on the tree, the birds of unrighteousness will devour and spoil it. In stripping a tree of its fruit, one of the first rules to be followed is that one must make a clean work of the area which he is able to reach from his place on the ladder; for once the ladder is removed to a different portion of the tree, any previously overlooked fruit must be left behind. There can be no profitable retracing of steps. A skilled picker, therefore, will always pivot on the ladder at every angle to insure that no fruit is being missed. He knows that he cannot return and retrace his steps. In like manner, each generation is required by God to pluck an area of the tree of God's providence, stripping and subduing the tree to the glory of God. And the basic rule which must here be followed is the same as that above: No surface of the tree must be left until one is finally certain that all accessible fruit has been plucked. Television is one of these fruits. It is ripe. It is promising. But if the children of light, in the anxiety of a heavenly perspective, refuse to pluck it, the children of darkness will devour it completely.

The loss of the fruit is serious enough. But the more serious matter is that God is displeased with His children. Since the Christian's works will be tried by fire, he would do well to discipline his attitude toward television. "If then you have not been faithful in the unrighteous mammon, who will entrust to you the true riches?" (Luke 16:11)

III

Savoir Faire, Please

On Thursday evening, May 5, 1949, television proudly unveiled its latent powers to quench a second craving in the breast of man, namely that of acquiring a satisfying *perspective* in life. On that night, video, in all its electronic glory, beamed out the first of twenty-six telecasts of General Eisenhower's classic documentary, *Crusade in Europe.* Based on authentic war films, taken by skilled Army, Navy, and Air Force photographers, the stirring story of the rise and fall of the Continental dictators was re-enacted on the television screen. Editorial work of the films was handled by the *March of Time.* Men in high journalistic and public relation posts were unanimous that *Crusade in Europe* was one of the biggest and proudest of television's early triumphs.

1. *The curious animal.* Personal experience teaches all of us that man is a curious as well as a laughing animal, for the disposition to inquire is as much a part of our normal life as eating and sleeping. Every man earnestly craves that warm feeling inside of him that he is in on the "know how" of living, that he has traveled widely, that he has seen much, that he has lived fully. When a neighbor can boast a possession of greater experience in the university of life than we can, what is at stake is not simply a balance in knowledge, but rather a contest in egos. One personality vies against the other for ascendancy.

Because of this competition between persons, each one of us, from early childhood through life, strives zealously to maintain his own social security. No closet is as intriguing to the child as that one into which entrance has specifically been forbidden by parents or elders. In adolescence, sex emerges as a new area of curiosity. Nor does this character bent in *Homo sapiens* terminate in adulthood, for there breathes no man who does not at times long for passage into the exotic, the romantic, the forbidden, the hidden. Notice the enthusiasm with which one responds to the challenge of chasing fire trucks or ambulances. To be first on a scene preserves egoistic pride. All revel in being the first to have some new information, or in being a "sidewalk superintendent" while a new building is in the process of construction. However trivial an insight into some new facet of life may be, if the ego is kept undisturbed through its acquisition, the social security of the individual is strengthened. As a constant diet, none want to admit that they are less informed on a topic than are their friends. Chronic confession is a difficult mood to live in.

Part of the power which urges man to find more information, security, and "know how" in life is a craving within us to be recognized and appreciated. Every individual is deeply desirous of keeping himself as socially and physically fit as possible. He enjoys being confided in. He thrives on applause and esteem. He devours recognition. Since variations of egoistic security, like mathematical combinations, are infinite, there is no conceivable end to their multiplication. Many people inwardly starve to be recognized and appreciated. In so slight a responsibility as giving information to strangers on how to cross town, for example, not a few find their egos being inflated. Having information or abilities which others lack is one positive way to keep the ego happy with itself.

2. *The universal disease*: *myopia*. While there are many maladies from which men suffer, no disease is so wide spread as that of myopia or shortsightedness. Every man is far too short-

sighted to suit himself. Bertrand Russell has wisely noted that many men wish they were God, and not a few have difficulty in persuading themselves that they are not. This sinful quest to be God is the most extreme outlet for man's urge to overcome the limitations of myopia.

Every man, whether he cares to or not, is forced to occupy an allotted area of space in the world. And he is destined to remain within that space a predestined span of time. Therefore, it is not part of his option either to leave this universe or to alter the decree that his days within it are threescore years and ten. Finite conditions are imposed upon man from birth. Over against this, however, God Almighty, who neither slumbers nor dies, is everywhere at the same time. God suffers from no myopia at all. His knowledge is infinite; His wisdom is perfect. No neighbor corrects the Almighty. No secrets are withheld from Him. While, therefore, God continues to enjoy absolute perspective by observing everything at once and from all possible points of view, human beings can only view a portion of reality at a time. This means that man is myopic in his vision.

The predicament of man is not unlike that of an ant, laboriously lugging a large bug across a plot of grass and remaining only vaguely conscious of either the distance already covered or the relation between the starting and ending points of the total journey. An ant's eye sees a blade of grass as a towering skyscraper and each yard of ground as a mile. For a person studying the ant from above, however, perception is a vastly easier thing. One who is suspended over the plot of grass in the hammock enjoys perspective. He can see at a glance the total relations involved in the ant's undertaking.

When judged in relation to the vastness of the universe, man is less than an ant. Spatially evaluated, he is no more than an insignificant, fraction of dust. Because of this handicap, man groans under the incumbency of myopia.

Yet, as a result of his power to direct, a freedom quite unknown to the ant, man can turn to his own industry to overcome shortsightedness. He may stand on the top of a mountain to see beyond. And when he meets problems involving data which lie above or below the threshold of his own field of sensation, instruments are invented to compensate the deficiency. Exhibit A of this is the 200-inch, camera-type telescope now reaching its final stage on Palomar Mountain in Southern California. The vast mirror is made of a gigantic, ribbed block of pyrex glass, nearly seventeen feet in diameter, thirty inches thick, and weighing almost fifteen tons. The immense camera is cradled in a framework of steel girders, with a combined weight of mirror, body, and cradle being over 500 tons. Having twice the diameter of the 100-inch instrument on Mount Wilson, and, accordingly, four times the light-gathering power, the Palomar telescope is expected to photograph faint stars lying twice the distance from the earth than was heretofore possible. Eight times the size of the volume of the universe than was previously possible will now be explored. An ingenious creature, this man!

Whether or not the prediction ever proves true that the Palomar telescope will give astrophysicists enough information to explain the physical origin of the universe, one thing is indubitably certain: When scientists have exhausted the potentialities of such a camera inside the atmosphere of the earth, every effort will be put forth to construct an outpost for research outside of that frame of reference — possibly on the moon. While there remains the slightest nook or cranny for man to explore, thus, *Homo sapiens* will not rest content with myopia. By every means possible the disease must be overcome.

The man on the street, however, has no easy access to such vast resources in overcoming his limitations. He must gain experience in his own modest way. And if he fails to find enough satisfaction alone, he projects himself into the place of others whose personal accomplishments have been unusual. The story of *Cinderella*, for example, has enraptured the hearts of thousands because the girl's experience symbolizes that release from social obscurity for which others earnestly crave. In an unexpected moment the moppet is given a chance to throw down her poverty and rags and take on the habit of a princess.

3. *TV: A perspective therapy.* With its electronic, magic wand, television can transform the forgotten man or woman, Cinderella-like, into a jeweled prince or princess in the world of imagination. Ready to respond to every beck and call of the televiewer are the nation's highest paid musicians, comedians, dramatists, composers, operatic stars, and showmen, asking nothing for their services beyond the cost of the electricity required to spark the television instrument itself. While only the rich previously were world wanderers, learning the fecundity of the earth's treasures, now even the poorest of men in TV areas can be whisked away from their parlor to the ringside of a world's championship tennis match or be borne on an elephant's back through the mysterious, inner recesses of fabulous India. In a television age, a war veteran, physically confined as a paraplegic, may now compete in world perspective with the wealthiest, most ambitious globe-trotter. If a thing can be seen with the eyes, television can relay it to the home.

Television foreshadowed some of its powers as a limitation-destroyer in the January, 1949 inauguration of Mr. Truman. A battery of television cameras, mounted along the line of procession and within the columned portico of the Capitol building, brought to the homes of thousands of televiewers up and down the eastern seaboard the thrilling details of the inaugural ceremonies. By alternating skillfully between close takes of the dignitaries in the line of procession and panoramic sweeps of the seas and seas of waiting people, the roaring of Air Corps planes and Navy blimp above, and the flawless step of the military, an unforgettable moment in the history of a great country was made visually accessible to the multitudes for the first time. While it is true that minor technical difficulties plagued the coverage from start to finish, a remarkably steady flow of history-making pictures were ground out. This early TV spunk prophesied some of the triumphs of the medium yet to come. But even more, it uncovered video's power to destroy myopia in man. No owner of television was too obscure that evening to share presidential honors, for the prince was Mr. Truman and the whole nation was Cinderella. All were invited to share the presidential box at the Inaugural Ball for a folksy, chatty evening. One competent authority has calculated that more Americans witnessed the inauguration of the President in 1949 than viewed the inaugurations of all the Presidents from George Washington to F.D.R. Again, hail to television!

If it is true that ninety per cent of our knowledge comes through the eye, television bids fair to be one of our greatest teachers of culture and language. Only a short time before the inaugural ceremonies in Washington, for example, TV marched boldly into the tradition-laden boxes of the Metropolitan Opera House for a telecast of Verdi's *Otello*. Hitherto the "Met" had been the exclusive monopoly of the privileged classes, a treasured experience in musical excellence planned and executed to meet the tastes of a special social caste, privately groomed for the experience. In true democratic fashion, video leveled off the audience, giving an equal place to the scullery maid with mop and bucket and the debutante in ermine. Someone remarked after the *Otello* spectacle that more opera fans saw and appreciated grand opera that one afternoon than could have come in person in half a score of entire seasons.

On a similar occasion Arturo Toscanini gave a superb TV performance by leading the NBC symphony. Every bead of perspiration, every intention in the maestro's face was faithfully relayed to the enthused music lovers. And late in the spring of 1949 KTTV of Los Angeles offered west-coast televiewers a literary treat. Shakespeare's *The Tragedy of Macbeth* was beamed out over television. Using eight different stages and three roving cameras, KTTV — in conjunction with the Pasadena Playhouse — took a lead in making great drama available to the masses of the people.

Charles C. Barry, vice-president in charge of television for the American Broadcasting Company, predicts that in video there will emerge the greatest force for understanding, education, entertainment, and participation in human affairs yet devised. This prophecy is guilty of no exaggeration. Wherever television has completed its initial bow it has surpassed even outside expectations. When full color is added, coupled with perfected screens and a nation-wide network of excellent stations, one can only gasp for breath to sum up TV's possibilities.

At the first appearance of television it was said that the new medium would "bring the world to man." A revision of this platitude is now in order. Television will "bring man to the world." The telephoto lens on the TV camera places the televiewer snugly beside the object of vision. Each televiewer is as close to the immediacy of moving reality as the miraculous lens of the video camera itself.

The films have long claimed the envied spot of being the nation's number one entertainment medium to shape the habits and preferences of the masses of the people. That glory (and responsibility) is now in the process of shifting over to television. Whatever the cinema can deliver, television can duplicate with vastly greater efficiency. Whereas a movie can be shown to but a few people at one time, television can unify a whole nation in one TV production. In telecasting daily news, for instance, video has already outstripped the cinema. Facing neither the time required to process film nor the aggravating period of waiting while a coordinated release is being syndicated, TV goes on the air at once, boasting an almost instantaneous coverage. News theaters are delaying their eventual death only by absorbing television itself into their movie schedules.

4. *Potential cultural increases.* While it certainly cannot be expected as an automatic blessing, one *theoretical* promise of television is that an enlarged cultural understanding, by the unification of new points of view, may be created; for used to its full height, video can unify the sympathies and understandings not only of friends assembled together in the living room, but also of the great continents themselves. If TV's potentialities are really exploited, misunderstandings between cultural centers, those suspicions which kindle the fires of war and aggression may be lessened. This will be a new gain for all.

International communications have previously been rapid, indeed, but only with video have the nations come into an immediate view of each other. This personal touch, for which there is no adequate substitute, is the perfect pre-condition for the cross-pollination of culture perspectives.

If an individual reveals his inward nature through *personality,* a social unit expresses its vitality through *culture.* Culture is the collective way in which a people rally to what they believe to be valuable in history. Culture is the totality of those customs, traditions, arts, and practices for the preservation of which a person may live and die. The Burmese have one type of culture and the British have another.

Cultural ties may be both good and bad, depending on how successfully the nation can segregate what is permanent in its national bonds from what is transient and temporary. Cultural vitalities are good when they serve as healthy rallying points for a nation's interests. A group, at best, is a very unwieldy mass. Its collective mind can be appealed to only through the rallying centers of universal loyalties: flags, freedom ideals, national anthems, historical events, great traditions, etc. Unless there is a unifying point for the freedom of a people, anarchy and tribal rebellion may threaten. A nation which has nothing to die for is a nation which has nothing to live for. The only way that the masses can unite their collective strength is by energetically responding to universal loyalties. When values are distributed among all members of a clan, collective powers are corralled. The nation cannot neglect its internal strength in times of peace, lest, when the hour of crisis comes, an aggressor, whose strength has been vitalized by loyalty programs, gains an easy access to the inner vitals of the nation's organism. Bands must play national anthems, holidays must be declared, and civil loyalties must be honored. A healthy culture is as valuable to the tribe or nation as is a good personality to the individual.

Cultural ties are an evil, however, whenever partial truths in national expressions are confused with timeless essences themselves. The true, good, and beautiful are changeless and absolute, but the relative ways in which parts of a culture express them are not. The two must be carefully distinguished if the worth of a cultural tie is to be segregated from its threatened evil There is no such expression as a *final* form of government, an *absolute* anthem, or a *flawless* calendar of state holidays or heroes. Cultural expressions are as temporal as the people who formulate them. In every social expression people think and act from the perspective of their own finitude, being motivated partially by the blinding rays of their own personal interests.

Whenever a limited cultural expression is confused with a finality, the threats of an overpowering nationalism, of which history is tragically replete, emerge. The German nation pitched itself headlong into World War II by being guilty of this fundamental fallacy in national life. *German* songs, *Ger-*

man philosophy, *German* poetry, and *German* dress, while being highly perfected indeed, were decreed final for all cultures. Believing that their form of nationalism enjoyed divine sanction, therefore, Hitler's troups fought fanatically to impose the German way of life upon non-Germanic cultures. The power of this false belief, so effectively fabricated by Hitler, narcotized the consciences of his troups into insensitivity as they spread sorrow and death across the length and breadth of the Continent. The German forgot that as long as man is both finite and egocentric, he will always alloy his cultural expression with the acid of a finite perspective.

Post-war Russia, over-intoxicated by its sudden emergence as a world power after centuries of obscurity, appears to be electing this same lethal path. Preaching that Communistic culture is a final "dialectical" expression of history, Russia resorts to force and violence to impose her ways upon the rest of the free world. She believes no means are unjustified, however bloody and violent, if the spread of the communistic ideology is increased. Since she contends that Russian nationalism has reached absolute maturity, it is not deemed necessary either to join other nations in the exchange of scholarship or to send delegates to the Olympic contests.

No nation is ever fully exempt from believing that its cultural pattern is a final one. An easy error into which most men tumble is to believe that their way of life is intrinsically superior to that of their neighboring land. When furloughed missionaries show moving pictures of how African tribes express themselves in cultural arts, for example, most people laugh. Whether they laugh out loud or hold it to themselves turns on how sensitive they are in maintaining their social respect. The weird costumes and the grotesque musical instruments used for the songs of the land seem so repulsive to the occidental mind. A thoughtful person quickly settles back into sobriety, however, when he is reminded by the missionary that the African way of life is beautiful and satisfying to that people and that our way of doing things is no less strange to the Africans.

Cultural prejudice is simply a bad habit, having not a scrap of justification in the real facts of life. Customs should be guided by God's standards of right and wrong, together with the personal taste of those involved. Within these termini there is room for endless variety. In this day of grace, one cultural expression ought never to be permitted to snuff out another. Crush a people and you crush the image of God. As long as we live by faith and not by sight, there must be an increase of sympathies between cultural expressions. Every man, being a sinner, judges from a finite perspective and according to personal interests. There are bound to be differences in nationalistic ties, therefore. History, geography, climate, and sanguineous ties will see to that.

Since nationalistic pride is but a bad habit, the best way to destroy that pride is to force a change in personal habits. Those who travel widely sense that becoming accustomed to the way other people do things is as simple as adjusting the self to different types of drinking water. It is the experience of all who journey from place to place that new water, when first drunk, tastes polluted. "There is no water like that at home!" so the story goes. But then, after a time of drinking this strange water, it slowly begins to taste more delicious than the old left behind. So in tasting cultures: By traveling widely and seeing how and why others live as they do, a broad-minded tolerance and sympathy are bred. An informed person places no final premium on either the way he dresses or the manner of decorum he follows when dining with others—so long as his habits do not transgress a law of God. He senses that etiquette is conditioned for the most part by the tastes of a particular people.

But how can a change of habits be forced on man? Is it feasible for half of the nation to board an ocean liner and travel around the world just to learn cultural sympathies? The answer to these questions is obvious. The man on the street, being economically chained to his post, cannot travel to gain perspective. What, then, can he do? The answer is lodged in television.

Video is the first effective invention which can economically and dramatically juxtapose the nations intimately one with another, so that international understanding, by the crisscrossing of cultural patterns, is made theoretically easier. Television will electronically transport a nation to the inmost seclusions of another, while yet guaranteeing to return the group for an early bedtime. The cinema, through its travelogue and "shorts" series, went far in this direction. But, as usual, its message was sporadic and interrupted. Television, if geared into international networks, can systematize the relations between continents. If it can succeed in making the customs of one nation the common knowledge of all other nations, it will assist greatly in the breakdown of narrow, unhealthy loyalties. If a person can only experience a thing long enough, often enough, foreign overtones will vanish and in its place a warm familiarity and understanding will germinate.

If television can seize its opportunities and make them good, the Christian will be first to rejoice. The Christian's marching order is love. But love is possible only when one has destroyed prejudice and pride in his own attitudes. The children of light, therefore, must not depreciate television's powers to increase social virtue. While only faith in Christ can finally bring about an understanding between the nations, one ought not to shun partial solutions. Until Christ is brought to the nations, one must respect whatever partially holds back the dike of international conflict.

5. *Release of the inner virtues.* One even dares to suggest that television, used in its best way, is able to draw out even the deepest, inner virtues in man.

Humility is the converse of pride. If pride comes when one thinks highly of himself, humility comes when one thinks little of himself. A humble man realizes that he is what he is by the grace of God. "What have you that you did not receive? If then you received it, why do you boast as if it were not a gift?" (I Corinthians 4:7) As long as a person evaluates himself by himself, he is easily deluded into thinking that he is somebody. But when he measures himself by the law of God, he suddenly discovers that he is really very small in his own strength. It is the sophomore in college, not the matured graduate student, who parades a claim to possessing great knowledge. A beginner in linguistics boasts of his great learning, while the master of many languages protests that he hardly knows even his native tongue. No more perfect criterion of ignorance could be devised, thus, than the test of pride. No *honest* man can be aware of the holiness, immensity, and sovereignty of God, on the one hand, and of the grossness of the created universe, on the other, without feeling the arrow of humility pierce his proud heart. When it is recalled all there remains to be known, Edison's remark that "We don't know one-millionth of one percent about anything," is surely well taken.

In its ideal powers TV may break down pride by introducing into the life of the individual some of the problems of others. Here—where human beings live and move and have their being—is where a real tug on the hearts of men can be begun.

An illustration will quickly clinch the point. Early in April, 1949, in the town of San Marino, California, an awful tragedy happened, sending the hearts of the entire nation racing with anxiety and hope. While innocently romping across the fields, scurrying with other children in the neighborhood, little Kathy Fiscus, aged three, slipped into the open mouth of an abandoned and since forgotten water well. Out of the darkness the little tot cried. The parents, frantic to know how to assist, summoned professional help. Within a matter of minutes police and ambulance cars screamed to the scene of the disaster. Painstaking efforts to seize the child with a long rope failed, however, and it was sensed then that more skilled help would be required. Cooperating fully, radio stations in Los Angeles beamed out urgent cries for assistance from professional "sand hogs" and well diggers. The response from this corps of laboring men was immediate and gratifying. Hundreds of thousands of dollars worth of heavy equipment lumbered into the field where little Kathy lay entombed, all of which was donated for the mercy work. And included among this gear was the portable mobile unit of video station KTTV, Los Angeles. When the television signal was clear, "operations rescue," as the effort was later labeled, was beamed out to waiting televiewers in Southern California. KTTV made television history by relaying the first on-the-spot telecast of a national tragedy. Unknowingly it had moved into what proved to be one of the most dramatic rescue attempts in American history.

Television turned the homes of thousands of Angelenos into altars of repentance and hope. So tense was the atmosphere in the Los Angeles area that little children, unable to sleep from watching the telecast, wept bitterly for Kathy; while their elders sat around grim, lump in throat, hoping against hope that somehow the rescue operations would end with an optimistic note and that the little girl would emerge from her ninety-foot tomb alive. Countless televiewers sat through whole nights, watching the operations, taking only what nourishment they had at hand. The television screen showed the giant clamshell shovels as they clawed angrily at the ground. Sweaty, tired workers risked every security to unlock the grave of the little girl. Video cameras caught the bewildered facial expressions of the twelve thousand odd subdued people who jammed outside of the temporarily constructed fences, keeping vigil night and day. Hundreds of TV owners testified that it had been years since their own souls had been so broken up by an emotional experience. God was so near to them. Prayer was so natural and easy as they joined hearts with that of the dying girl.

The nerves of those Californians who studied the "operations rescue" over television did not begin to calm down until Sunday evening, over fifty hours after the tot disappeared down the rusty well shaft, when the family doctor, faithful to the end, painfully announced that little Kathy was dead. Although deep in grief, the entire world sighed with relief that the girl's sufferings were over. But no eyes were as wet as those who either saw the operations personally or who witnessed it through the television lens. Parents imagined it was their own child in the pit. Children felt themselves in the tomb. No radio description of the rescue could ever have matched the vividness of the telecast.

Man is a very peculiar creature in many ways. But one of the strangest, one of the most inexplicable, is the inconsistent and peculiar way in which he reacts to the details of tragedy. When a person sees in the daily paper that fifty thousand Chinese have perished in an earthquake, for example, he simply sighs momentarily, superficially gives his best blessings to the survivors, and then hastily turns to the funnies. This is one side to the enigma of man's nature. But if his doorbell suddenly rings and there enters a frightened, weeping neighbor who pleads for him to call an ambulance, since her child has just drowned in their back yard pool, then an almost uncontrolled anxiety overtakes him. Although only a single life has been lost in the one instance, in stark contrast to the unspeakable tragedy of fifty thousand in the other, the proximity of the one accident to the daily life of the man puts the incident in a new framework of vividness. This is the enigma: If the bitter side to the human drama is not dumped right on a man's lap, he will aloofly by-pass it every time. In utter complacency one can snap his finger at the sorrows and calamities of an entire nation, providing it is far enough out of his reach, while being thrown down into the throes of despair when a minor calamity strikes in his own household. One's own headache seems so much more vivid than the leprosy of a distant one.

The children of light have long been sensitive to this anomaly in sinful nature. In hours of peace and tranquility, when one's health is fine and his income steady, the foreboding warning of God's judgment to come seems no more important to man than the twitter of distant sparrows. But when sickness overtakes him, when poverty haunts the family circle, when death overshadows, then the gospel minister, who previously had been smiled at, is hastily summoned for a last-minute effort to put one's house in order. Because of this paradox in man's depraved nature, Christian workers find it exceedingly difficult to warn men of darkness while it is still light. Their predicament is parallel to that of the chaplain during the period of war. When the army games are on and the din of battle is far away, the chaplain's call to righteousness falls on unsympathetic ears. But when the fright of zero hour, minus one, arrives and the sound of guns is at hand, prayer and stillness before God suddenly assume new and unexpected worth.

This character weakness spreads out over most of the decisive life of man. High school students, for example, while being fully warned against leaving the halls of learning to marry or take employment, flee from learning, despite all, only to reap an inevitable harvest of frustration and inferiority. Tragedy is vivid when it actually is faced, but up until that time it seems most inconsequential. Sin blinds a man to a rational scale of values. Inevitable, future sorrow is lightly treated, while an immediate stomach-ache receives earnest attention. Every drunkard regrets drunkenness when its ills take their heavy toll on his life, but the first glass is cheerfully taken when inebriation seems far away.

One of the most regrettable fruits of this deficiency is that many of the finest and richest decencies in man remain concealed beneath a rough-and-ready complacency over things just as they come along. Inner decencies are sometimes drawn out only by a tragedy. Coarse and rough men, who otherwise feed on profanity and suggestiveness, are melted down, like butter in the sun, when they stand beside the coffin of one whom they love. Such men were always capable of showing tenderness and concern for the lovelier things in life, but their potential virtues lay unaccented until circumstances forced them out. All men have a gold vein of social decencies in their heart which is very rarely mined. Total depravity may prevent a man having any goodness before God, but it does not for a moment cancel out the virtues of social good.

The uniqueness of man is seen once again. Man is a sympathetic as well as a laughing and curious animal. The dog exhibits certain reflex responses as it whines over the dead carcass of its companion, but only man can rise to an empathic response. Empathy is that feeling of sympathy which one has when he imaginatively puts himself in the place of another. When a factory worker is caught in the moving gears of a machine, being slowly drawn to inevitable death, fellow workers, having knit their hearts to that of the dying man through the bonds of love and sympathy, sense the pain of the other with a vividness equal only to passing through that death themselves.

Through empathy they exchange their own freedom for the suffering of their friend, taking on his grief in their person. Through some mysterious power man is able to unite the inner recesses of his heart to that of others, making their experiences his own, taking their cross upon himself. At the funeral, therefore, it is man, not the flowers or the chairs, which weeps. And no animal accidentally present would sob. Man's nature alone is a compound of freedom and spirit. "For what person knows a man's thoughts except the spirit of man which is in him?" (I Corinthians 2:11)

Love, the highest of the Christian virtues, is intimately related to sympathetic virtues. A man is in love only when he places himself and his own security in a subordinate relation to the security and safety of another. "Love does not insist on its own way." (I Corinthians 13:5) If she could relieve the pain of suffering in a child, the mother would many times over take the disease upon herself; or, if it would help, she would even thrust her own arm into the fires to be burned for the sake of the little one. Love is possible only because of the sympathetic strands in man's freedom.

Since love is the finest and highest expression of selfless concern, Christianity, having as its foundation stone the law of love, has been declared by western culture the final religion. Christ appeals to men in terms of their *outside* possibilities as free spirits, not to any paltry or compromised virtuosity which may exercise only part of man's nature. In Christ's teachings, sin is the lack of love. The law requires perfect love for God and one's neighbor.

Being capable of love and sympathy (by God's grace), and yet by allowing these virtues to remain dormant and concealed most of the time, man mediates the same contradiction in his person as does the person who walks the streets in dire poverty, while all the while concealing a vast fortune of money hid beneath his mattress or sewed in a coat lining. All agree that when a rich man lives like a pauper, he is an object of pity; but few sense the pity due him who, while capable of endless love for God and man, seldom taps these treasures, living only for sin and self. All men crave happiness, but who is so bold to think that the world will ever have it perfectly until men seek God with all their heart and their neighbor's security as their own? If every man who is capable of selflessness were to live on that high level, the kingdom of God would be in our midst in fact as well as promise.

The sum of the matter is this: Television, by removing man from the narrow field of self-defined interests, is capable of teaching what it means to be fully man. If the quickest entrance to life's tragedies comes through the eyes, and if video has united sight with sound, then one can rightfully require the medium to discharge its responsibility to teach men to cry as well as laugh. Ideally directed, TV can move man out of his sinful isolation and place him face to face with the world outside where the barbed and thorny human drama is being played. The fifty thousand Chinese who perish in an earthquake will become neighbors in tragedy when the telephoto lens of the television camera catch the dying looks on the faces of the trapped. The blood on a Calcutta or Bern pavement will be blood in the living room. The halfhearted and complacent, whisked off to see the German concentration camps, can be brought next to the baseness of what remains when a nation corrupts the law of God. Skillfully employed, television can make the real world so vivid to those who would prefer to rest at ease in Zion, that much of the excuse for disconcern will be neutralized. Time and space narcotize men into stupor. If tragedy is temporally or spatially far enough away, it concerns one but slightly. Television will revoke this anesthesia and put in its place the realism of things as they actually are.

It would be optimistic to think for one moment that this television age will be one of love, however. Hardly. Potentialities do not always convert into actualities. Television magnates may jam their video hours with all sorts of unworthy programs, by-passing completely all responsibility to elicit love and empathy in man. That is one fact. Another is that even where there are good programs, the televiewer himself may either turn to another, and less wholesome, station or even snap the set off entirely. That is another fact. And then there is the datum that people at times become so calcified in their sin that not even the nearest vision of tragedy affects them. In fact, the sadist glories in the grief of others. Those who planned and executed the brutalities in World War II, for example, having passed outside of the zones of human decency itself, showed every symptom of being confirmed in wickedness. The sufferings of others are but a sparkling cocktail to their lips.

Television, however, can increase an exposure of those human situations out of which ideally there may emerge a deeper accentuation of love and sympathy. For the rank and file, TV may make a difference in the way they live. Most men are more than ready to weep with those that weep.

At this point a note of warning to the children of light must be injected, lest a perfectionistic ideal be used as a fulcrum in removing the edge of the above argument. The righteous, realizing correctly that final love, final empathy, can come only when one is under the saving, strengthening graces of the Lord Jesus Christ, may conclude, quite incorrectly, that all means which effect but a partial release of man's inner virtues are neither to be acknowledged nor encouraged. Here, as elsewhere, the children of light must become realistic, lest they be less wise in their own generation than the children of this age. We may hope for cake, but if we are hungry enough even a crust of bread will be received with thanksgiving. The children of light, in their earnest concern to direct men to heaven, must not become blinded to their role as the "salt of the earth." They are to savor and preserve the earth, not spoil and putrify it. If a pagan psychiatrist, therefore, one who has never known the Lord, is able to bring a partial normalcy to a distorted mind, encouraging that person to move into the peace of a balanced, decent life, such a therapy, though it falls far short of the ultimate answer for men, is nevertheless a good which must be recognized and appreciated by the children of light. In a mixed society, where tensions mount by the hour and where explosion and revolution are being flirted with by unregenerate men, a prudent man will give thanks for any arms which are thrust in the dike. The children of light are wise in not believing that partial answers are the final answers, but they are foolish when they become blinded to the partial truth in partial answers.

If one will only grant the point that television has powers and that these powers can be used for the good, he will grasp at once the endless ways in which the new medium's potentialities can be exploited.

Civic, social, and mercy agencies — ever alert to new ways of opening up the hearts (and pocketbooks) of men — ought to cast a careful eye in the direction of television. If the tragic end of those who spurn the law of God is made part of an F.B.I. presentation, children, toying with the initial thrill of rebellion and lawlessness, may be influenced to follow the right before plunging headlong into tragedy. "Until I went into the sanctuary of God; then understood I their end. Surely thou didst set them in slippery places: thou castedst them down into destruction. How are they brought into desolation as in a moment!" (Psalm 73:17-19) All mature men know that "the weed of crime bears bitter fruit," but the problem is how to show it to those immature minds who may turn to crime. TV should shoulder part of this responsibility. On the wings of video the bitter fruits of crime can be borne into the living room for public exhibition. The electric chair will be a more fearful symbol of justice for the potential criminal when publicly displayed in its full awe.

The ways which social groups can employ television are as endless as combinations of notes on the piano. Would not the sale of veteran's poppies increase manyfold, for example, if a life-sized TV screen portrayed the sorrowful confinement of a live paraplegic to others passing by with the indifference of the Levite going from Jerusalem to Jericho? The distance between the veteran as a person and the poppy as a symbol is too great. The suffering man is just like the fifty thousand Chinese — too far away and too removed from the vividness of daily life to gain much attention. It is only when one walks through a veteran's hospital and learns from experience what the rows of beds mean, that he is shaken from his lethargy and made sympathetic inside for these who fought and *almost* died for their country. But not all have access to hospitals. Television must eliminate this deficiency by putting the reality of suffering on the corner of Main and Superior Streets in every U. S. city. If TV will create an intimacy between the sufferer and the healthy, new vitalities of sympathy and generosity will be forthcoming.

This principle of reducing the distance between sorrow and the world is being exploited with great success by polio societies. By bearing around the country a live victim in an iron lung, people are given an opportunity to see firsthand how death is temporarily defied through science. As the lines and lines of curious people pass by the girl in the iron lung, they begin to grasp through experience what it means so to be confined. Realizing that they might some day be in that same condition, and being emphatically able to enter into the sufferings of the individual in the lung, they find themselves unlatching the strings of their purses much more easily than if they had heard only a radio appeal for the same cause. In immediacy there is sympathy.

War relief agencies can televise the nature and extent of the suffering which accompanies international conflict. The aftermath of war can be exhibited in the living room of the spared. Alcoholics Anonymous will be presented a new sword for its noble fight against the dreaded powers of alcohol. The end of those who lose self-control can be televised, together with the mechanics to be followed in gaining self-control.

Let video go to the courtroom and show the shattered end product of a boy or girl who sells out to sin, outraging the image of God within him. Let the telephoto TV lens punctuate the gospel warning that the wages of sin is death. Follow the path of the derelict in Skid Row, and let the sorrow in his eye as he senses the disgrace he is, both to himself and to his loved ones, be its own sermon.

In short, looking for social decency in man is like drilling for water: it can be found if one digs deep enough. Let us engage television to assist in the drilling! Our generation will have discharged its obligation to the new medium only **if it has** faith in its ideal, outside possibilities for good.

IV

Read the Label and See for Yourselves

The final, yet somewhat overlapping, virtue which television may deposit for good in our generation is to stimulate a wider interest in *education*.

1. *The two types of knowledge.* The following question was recently posed to a number of people: "If you were obliged to make a decision between parting with your faculty of hearing or with that of seeing, which would you be willing to lose first?" In each case — with no exceptions recorded — the answer immediately came that the faculty of hearing would have to go first. It is a heavy cross to live in the silent valley of the deaf, but to stumble through an endless sky of darkness is the first step to death itself. Surely, therefore, no small truth is embodied in the optometrist's creed: "Next to life itself, our most gracious gift is sight."

When one remembers the truth of the Chinese proverb that one picture is worth ten thousand words, it is not difficult to appreciate why light is our most efficient medium of knowledge. Compare, as a simple illustration, the difference between the mountain of words needed to describe the contents of a room with the easy way which the eye absorbs the room's relations in a simple glance. In one panoramic sweep the eye blots up faint and rich outlines alike.

The reason why sight is so valuable a faculty, thus, is because it gives us immediate, vivid experience. It is common knowledge that the richest, the most satisfying, way to gain knowledge of something is to experience it personally. Second-hand knowledge, while it may be true and valuable information, is never as striking as the immediacy of a personal encounter. Theoretical knowledge about a kiss may bring a person a long way toward understanding both the meaning of the kiss and the attributes which distinguish it from other experiences; but to feel the full significance of the flowing together of loving personalities, one must enjoy the intimacy of the kiss for himself. So, in all areas where personal experience is possible. The plunge into cold water brings a shock and refreshment which are never quite captured in words. A poetic description of the sunset, while enrapturing and delighting, comes far short of the fecundity gained by standing on the summit of a hill, personally drinking in the glorious hues of that descending ball. The Queen of Sheba, though she had heard reliable reports of the glories of King Solomon, released ejaculations of joy that "the half was not told" only when she personally inspected the fabulousness of that great man's kingdom for herself.

If one will reflect on what has been just said, he will realize immediately that there are basically two types of knowledge in the world: one is gained by direct experience, while the other comes through the testimony of others. Both are valid. Both are needed. But both are not equal in imagery power. Direct experience transpires in a depth of personal experience unknown to the indirect.

Philosophers have given the names "knowledge by acquaintance" and "knowledge about" to these fields of direct and indirect experience respectively. Let us examine these, seeking to appreciate the powerful way in which television can become a one-man university in our generation.

If, after reading or hearing about the city called Paris, we believe there actually is such a place, then we have "knowledge about." We may have never personally visited the metropolis for ourselves hitherto. But we are still firmly convinced that there is such a city.

If, however, Uncle Harry leaves us a fortune and, lo, we depart on a world cruise which finally includes a visit to Paris, then our "knowledge about" is transmuted into "knowledge by acquaintance." We become no more assured that there is such a city, after we have been there; yet, something inside of us has changed. As in eating a pear, going through an automobile accident, or drinking a cool glass of water, a thrilling depth to our experience has been added. Paris, which we always knew existed, is now a Paris which we know for ourselves. It is a Paris on whose streets we have walked. A Paris in whose street cafes we have eaten. A Paris where we first tried out our little knowledge of French. It is the same Paris — yet it is not. It is now *our* Paris.

Since it has the power to remove an individual from the limitations of his own home and put him against the world outside, TV's educational potentialities are immense. It can forge a closely simulated "knowledge by experience."

It is quite true that nothing can exactly match either the vividness of personality being in World War II or the pain connected with having one's own foot being crushed by an elevator. Television in this sense is not strictly a perfect counterpart to "knowledge by experience." Nevertheless, the experience in watching television comes so close to "knowledge by experience," that for all practical purposes one may claim to be right on the spot when a television show is beamed to him. The "plus" or "minus" differences between the television show and actual experience are negligible.

Television's telephoto lens are, in fact, able to transport the televiewer even closer to the scene of life than he would ordinarily be able to effect by himself. The camera can jump fences to move right up to the racing automobile. And television will take the nation with it.

It does not require a great deal of imagination to sense that video is a colossal giant of an instructor. The ingenuity of science, alas! has made it possible for all men to enjoy the rich immediacy of life. It has put a magic carpet in every living room, an Aladdin's Lamp over every hearth. How grateful one ought to be, therefore, that he has been privileged to live in the television age!

To illustrate TV's educational facilities one need only imagine a proposed telecast of an international flower show. Let us presuppose, for the sake of illustration, that full color in television is already a common possession. At first glance it would seem that the one who personally visits the flower show enjoys a perspective far exceeding that which the poor televiewer in his own home has; but a more cautious judgment exposes the superficiality of the advantage. When one looks at the flowers in person, he is limited in what he can see by the extent of his own small appreciation of flowers. He can see no more than his own field of appreciation can take in. In contrast to this lone-wolf pursuit of nature's beauty, the televiewer will have at his access the combined skills of several trained technicians, together with botanical experts to provide commentary for the roving cameras. From a multiplicity of angles the cameras will pour pictures into the waiting mobile unit stationed outside the exhibit. Turreted lens will alternate between distant and close view shots as easily as tilting for over or under views. What will flow into the home of the televiewer, sitting munching bon bons, is a steady stream of color movies of excellent critical composition. Only rarely could the experience be duplicated by one's attempt to understand the flower show from his own perspective. Types and history of flowers, information which could never be printed on all of the exhibits, will be sent over television to the televiewer.

In a sense, television may even improve on real life. Improvement is always the work of the artist. He seeks to sum up the excellent and beautiful in life, leaving out whatever might detract from the symmetry of the whole. If two heads are better than one, as the platitude has it, will not many TV heads be better than one in interpreting life?

Wherever television cameras are pointed, an incomparable depth of "knowledge by experience" is created. A novelist, limited to words in constructing expression, must devote endless pages building up a description of his main characters. The television scenarist, however, can leave that matter almost entirely to the camera. With one glance the televiewer can identify the villain's malicious mouth and black mustache for himself. And if this is not enough to establish the scoundrel's character, a few words from gravel-like throat will finish it off. Video, in short, enjoys the same educational advantages as the cinema, plus owning the agility, economy, and catholicity of radio.

2. *The limitations of institutionalized education.* Since high school, university, and specialized institutions rest their curricula on educational presuppositions which make but a limited use of "knowledge by acquaintance," there is little reason to suppose that TV will introduce any startling alterations in its stated program. While this may appear at first glance to be a pessimistic conclusion, one must remember that television, like all mediums, has its limitations as well as its potentialities. Like the radio and the cinema, TV will remain primarily an entertainment and education medium for the masses of the people. One goes to school primarily to grow in "knowledge about." The application of television to university life, therefore, must remain at best but a by-product of the broader purposes of the medium.

The immense costs of producing live television programs excludes the practical employment of TV for teaching those arts and sciences which can be learned from books. Since gifts to private institutions are already on the decline, due in part to the large inheritance and income tax levies, large bequests are becoming more and more conspicuous for their absence. Even state supported schools will meet a difficulty in budgeting the luxury of television education.

Television will probably sound only a minor note in the school curriculum, likewise, because it is basically an evening medium. Furthermore, the rigid schedule on which a school operates will lessen the formal contribution of video to education. A moral agreement binds students and faculty together. They agree to abide by the stringencies of a common schedule. The plasticity of television can be absorbed into this iron-clad arrangement only by way of exception.

But the most profound reason why TV will have but a small place in institutional education is that its search is primarily for other than "knowledge by acquaintance." Most of what is taught in the schools lends itself solely to "knowledge about." Because of their theoretic nature, therefore, "reading, 'riting, and 'rithmetic" are, to put it mildly, not very telegenic. At least, no advertiser is going to pay a premium price for a telecast to teach disciplines which can be handled with equal, or greater, facility by a slate chalk board and a schoolteacher. The advertiser wants to sell his products. Hence, he must appeal to the interests of the masses. And the last thing that the multitudes want is to be subjected to formal education. They want to be entertained, that and nothing else. If the populace is going to be educated by television, it will have to receive it in heavily coated sugar pills.

A university is founded on two main pillars: a good library and competent instructors. Visual education will never replace either of these ingredients of higher education. A book is easy to manufacture. It is portable. And it is highly communicative of knowledge. Unlike a finished telecast, a book can be read over and over. It can be taken under the student's arm and made his possession for review and study in the years which lie ahead.

While it is true that the movies have had an immense effect upon the manners and morals of the university students, it is not true that the cinema has made much of a contribution to the educational program of the university life. It is not because the movies are not excellent at conveying knowledge, nor is it that their propaganda power is surpassable. Rather, the reason is that the higher one climbs the ladder of higher learning, the less "knowledge by acquaintance" satisfies as a vehicle of learning. Advanced studies are practically pure abstractions, not yielding to the limitations of spatial dimensions. How, for example, could one televise the mathematical maze of Whitehead and Russell's *Principia Mathematica* or the philosophical complexities of Aristotle's *Metaphysics?* And yet these exact, technical documents, and a million others like them, constitute the Gibraltar of any advanced graduate school. Video need not frighten the college librarian into thinking that her job is insecure, therefore, for one of the proudest glories of man is, and ever shall be, the art of mastering abstractions. And abstractions require books for their permanent recording.

On the positive side of the balance sheet, however, there are an endless number of ways in which "knowledge by acquaintance," *still the most vivid way of learning spatial relations,* can be absorbed by formal education. Events of national significance can momentarily unify the entire student body in the land: A presidential election, an international incident, a great geographical discovery, a national tragedy. Rich blood can be pumped into what might otherwise remain a lifeless course of government. The entire class will be privileged to sit before a television set and see first hand the Congress of the United States debate those technical transactions in goverment which will make such a difference to the future of our land. This will spread a healthy nationalism among even those remote rural schools which have never been able to afford the luxuries of, say, a field trip to Washington, D. C. All of the departments of government can now be spread out by television for the entire nation to see and appreciate.

Vocational techniques will be a "natural" over television. For years now television has competed with the conventional observation-room method for medical students to watch a surgical operation. Students and visiting doctors now relax in lounge chairs in a near-by room, watching the hand of the surgeon perform the operation and listening to his description as he proceeds. A sensitive TV camera, mounted above the field of operation, beams the performance to others. Formerly six or seven feet separated the medic from the locus of operation, but now, with the displacement of the observation platform, the student's eye is as close to the patient as the physician himself. And, as a nice historical highlight, medical doctors were among the first to enjoy a public preview of color television. Dr. George L. Hoffman of the University of Pennsylvania Hospital, after watching a telecast of an obstetrical performance, declared that color television is the most beautiful thing he had ever seen.

Television can serve as an extra pair of eyes for a person in numerous ways. For example, psychology understands very little about either undisturbed infant reactions or human response in the face of death. A distant television set, mounted with telephoto lens, can now record such reactions for the advancement of knowledge. Because the camera can be set at a distance from the subject, the latter will be quite unaware that it is being watched. Again, a television camera can be mounted in an area of dangerous chemicals or electricity, such as in the work on atomic energy, so that the engineer, without risking his own safety, can have a close-in view of his lethal field of work. By television the plant foreman may keep before him a quick picture of the operations in any part of the factory. Woe, now, to those who loiter on the job!

The United States Navy uses television in the mass training of its new enlistees. At the Navy Television Studio at Port Washington, New York, studio telecasts beam simulated plane and gun battles to the ordnance and gunnery students at Merchant Marine Academy, Kings Point, a distance of four and seven-tenths miles away. Simultaneity of observation, without sacrificing individualized attention, is accomplished by the magical television set.

Time would fail to outline the potentialities of video in other forms of industry. A small amount of ingenuity will furnish the employer a multitude of outlets. Methods in the art of smelting ore, of operating an assembly line in an automobile plant, of mining copper rock, or a million other techniques in industry can instantly be transferred from the pit or furnace to the eager apprentice in the factory schools. Once again TV has an excellent chance of surpassing the success which even the movies enjoyed in the technological trade schools. While the movies are "canned," a time elapsing between their filming and their showing, television is live. TV can show how progress stands at the mouth of a roaring blast furnace at the exact time in which the class is meeting. This instantaneousness will strengthen student morale. A person is much more thrilled at being "on the spot" than in being told that what he is watching is simply a movie-lot caricature.

A lively debate is now in progress, and will continue for some time to come, to discover whether TV will increase or decrease the nation's cultural standards. The answer is that only time can tell, for trends can move up or down, depending on the criteria which television men elect to follow in their programming. Video is a power either to cure or corrupt. All turns on how it is used. If it is directed by those who cherish the finer things of life, it can increase the speech habits of the nation. People naturally pattern their manner of speaking after their so-called stage heroes or heroines. But if video is permitted to slide into carelessness on matters of speech and literary standards (the more likely possibility), then a general decline in the cultural standards of the nation will probably follow.

A similar conflict will rage in all of the arts. Good literature can be televised only when station masters become meticulous in costume, setting, and dialogue. But if carelessness marks the caliber of their productions, a decline in the tastes of the nation will result. Experiments in Great Books forums have been tried, for instance. The reaction of some of the TV stations is that a popular, carnival type of forum is preferred to the academic or literary method. This trend suggests one of the dangers in making audience interest the sole guide in telecasting. Unless an effort is made to lift, not simply conform to, the tastes of the nation, decline will very likely set in. The course of least resistance, naturally, is to lean to the coarse, the vulgar, and the burlesque, not to the fine, the endearing, and the ennobling.

3. *Mass education.* When the circle of discussion over the educational possibilities of television is completed, we find ourselves right back where we started. Whatever ancillary role TV may play in formal, institutionalized education, its undisputed value still lies in the education of the multitudes of the people, those who revolt from the mere thought of a bookish education.

The masses in any society must never be underestimated, as if they form simply a social class which is only to be tolerated, but not recognized or encouraged. The Phi Beta Kappa has an incomparably important part to fulfill in drawing up the blueprints of history's course; but such a scholar enjoys the leisure of his meditation only because the rank and file of men dig coal, wait on tables, and process chemicals. The man on the street, thus, is a pretty important fellow! He also controls the votes which make great turns in the nation's history. Now, it is this average man, "John Q. Public," who, obtaining his education from the university of life, will do much of his graduate work perched in front of a television set. This proverbial "John" wants to be educated, indeed; he wants to have his *savoir faire* and perspective increased. But what he does not want to submit to is a formal, bookish method of training. He cannot sit still long enough for that. He cannot keep his mind on abstractions. His education has to be one without texts, assignments, tuition, examinations. His education must be dramatic, colorful, and painless. The man on the street is still a curious animal, but not so curious as to study a technical treatise on either engineering or the existence of God. Demanding an effortless education, therefore, it is not surprising to see him turn to the radio, movies, and television for data. Filled with stories and pictures, these mediums pump knowledge into him effortlessly.

Television is the perfect professor to the masses. The living room is the classroom, and the whole range of dramas, movies, documentaries, debates, athletic contests, etc., make up the professor's lectures. This type of classroom, one in which the rank and file need just sit in an overstuffed chair with slippers on, is "just what the doctor ordered."

Since it is bound to control much of the advertising of the nation, TV will proceed a long way in dictating the purchasing habits of the masses. The goal of the advertiser is so to shape the habit expectancy of the individual, that when he walks through a department store or grocery market and sees the mountains of merchandise, his habit patterns lead him intuitively to the products advertised. Advertising, thus, is an accomplished science, an art which follows the latest psychological reports on the behavior of man.

Television is the advertiser's dream. TV is, in fact, a *sales*, rather than just an advertising medium. It combines the virtues of the movies, radio, house-to-house calling, and the billboard. Perhaps the most convincing illustration of the sales powers of television is the "moppets' stampede" which descended upon department stores soon after video came into its own. Being unable to obtain better movies, TV men revived hundreds of old fashioned "horse operas" for television hours. As a result of this coverage, Western gear immediately became a fad among that younger set which idolized such spurs as William Boyd (Hopalong Cassidy), Roy Rogers, and Gene Autry. Television swiftly turned items of slow sales into a million-dollar industry. Across the land children eagerly purchased hand-tooled leather goods, hand-embroidered gabardine shirts, cowboy hats, pajamas, shirts, guns, hats, sombreros, cuffs, lariats, and dozens of other items for the range. Sales galloped under the impetus of this stampede!

Because of their box office standards the movies have, with but minor exceptions, excluded advertising from the screens. Some local theaters have accepted advertisements, but that only to keep their houses from going in the red. Radio has been showered with millions of advertising dollars in years past. In fact, people have heard so much pleading on the radio that they are not a little weary of it. Despite its dexterity, however, the radio is limited to verbs, nouns, and adjectives. The billboard gave a full picture of the product, a virtue absent in radio. But then, the billboard could not speak. In house-to-house calling the ideal type of advertising was found. The product could be shown and demonstrated, thus lessening sales resistance to a minimum. But the method is too limited, too expensive.

Only television has been able to scoop together all of the contributing ingredients of the other mediums and wed them in one grand outlet. Uniting their best features, it will escort the televiewer personally into the steak or cheese house to see the fresh cuts for himself. A golden-voiced commentator will be on hand to add spice and season to sales pleas. Video will avoid the offense which the salesman at the door risked. Out of an enthusiasm to sell his product he was often tempted to be more bold than he ought. Human nature is such that people will rebel when they have the faintest inkling that they are being forced into action. Television will not as much as softly rap at the door. The advertiser will suddenly appear at the end of a newscast to announce pleasantly the virtues of the product he is trying to sell. Telecommercials will, when they come to maturity, be laid out on that same entertaining level as the thrilling teledrama which precedes them. Much of the crude abruptness faced by radio will thereby be spared. One may not care about smoking, yet he cannot but be impressed with the ingenuity of the Lucky Strike cartoon with its battalion of animated, marching cigarettes. By studying such ingenuity one can begin to realize what the art of advertising, given some real thought in preparation, is capable of performing in TV. Television is a subtle sales medium, indeed. The masses of the people, whether they drink or not, will find their front room jammed with beer salesmen vying with one another to tell fifty-five reasons why one's tastes will be so much more satisfied with one brand rather than another. Powers for good are also powers for bad!

Advertising is only the beginning of the graduate course of the masses, however. Video must beam a simple, entertaining story of our nation, for example. America is a democratic land, a country in which each individual, being made in the image of God and endowed with the inalienable rights of "life, liberty, and the pursuit of happiness," is called upon to shoulder a share of the responsibility in the control and management of its government. The federal government is never an end in itself. Its sole justification for existence is in being a servant of the people who make up a mixed society. Where there are good and bad together in society, government is needed as a praise for the good and a terror to the evil. It follows from this that there is probably no place on earth where the electorate must be more enlightened than in a democracy, for it is the majority which arbitrate between the contesting parties seeking the rule of the land. A poor or hasty choice of leadership may only end in the dissolution of that very historical continuity for the preservation of which the great forefathers of our land lived and died. A dictator can corrupt both the people and the nation overnight. One ought to remember the sagacious insight of William Randolph Hearst: "Good government in a democracy depends upon the enlightenment of the electorate . . . They cannot vote right unless they are completely informed."

And yet what is a realistic solution to the problem of educating the masses of the people? The universities, despite all of their theoretic knowledge on the subject, cannot solve it, for it was out of an aversion to such bookish learning that the masses of the people terminated their formal education in the first place. John Q. Public will run in the other direction if a course in the "Theoretical Machinery of a Democratic Society" is announced. Something with a much more popular turn to it will have to reach this evasive individual. Formal education would long ago have enlightened the world if it had the capacity. Statistics show, however, that only a few actually go on to higher learning.

While the populace stubbornly refuse to enroll in a university, they nonetheless do learn a philosophy of life. They gain it from popular mediums as the newspaper, radio, cinema, group discussions, and, alas, television. "Public opinion" emerges from such a body of convictions, a power which politicians often fear more than God. Upon the shoulders of television will rest a great deal of the responsibility for shaping this public opinion. It is the most popular, the most effective medium for the mass communication of knowledge. No small responsibility lies on those who own or control TV, therefore. The destiny of our land turns upon the moral integrity of the masses. They make up our largest voting bloc. Television must popularly instruct the people in the meaning of government and their own relation to it. It must lift the social taste of the people by bringing fine arts into the home.

America is justly proud of the fact that many of its finest presidents have come from humble social backgrounds. In this land of plenty and opportunity television can go far in opening the dimmed eyes of the weak to their boundless opportunities here. By being shown what others with smaller opportunities have been able to accomplish, contemporary youth may have their own powers of ingenuity and imagination aroused. Hardly one man in ten exploits a fraction of the talents God has given him. Great numbers of young men in World War II, for example, drafted out of farm or shop, suddenly found themselves forced by the government to shoulder responsibilities and leadership for which they would never have dreamed they were qualified. Leaving the plow or the assembly line, they turned to servicing some part of the most immense war machine ever devised. The men were not a little surprised to discover what they were capable of perfoming once they set their minds to the task. After they had tasted the thrill of leadership and responsibility, they found it extremely unsatisfying to return to places of obscurity after the war. Armed by the same courage with which they fought the war, they entered education, business, and the clergy. The G. I., in fact, was the mainstay of the college for many years after the war.

War's horrors, however, are not compensated by the betterment of a few, for international conflict is too expensive a price to pay for such gains. Other more peaceful, less expensive, means should be set in motion to arouse man's potentialities. Once again, TV, while neither the whole nor perfect answer, is our solution. It can quickly expose the fallacy that one's social status is marked out for him before he is born by tracing out in the lives of others the real basis of social advance in a free society. The poor can learn how to gain economic stability, the neglected to earn recognition, and the careless to cultivate self-interest and personal pride. Since man is capable of rising to these virtues, television can both define them and show people how they, like others before them, can gain them. The negro or immigrant, who chafes under the delusion that white races are biologically superior to others and that non-whites are predestined to the inferiority of bondage, can be taught to realize that social gains are secured, not by superficial epidermal differences, but by the confidence, aptitude, and moral fiber of the individual himself. "If there is a will, there is a way." The populace needs vision, stimulus, courage. TV may assist in supplying them these virtues.

At this point, the warning of Gilbert Seldes, Director of Television Programs for the Columbia Broadcasting System should be injected. Writing in the *Atlantic Monthly,* Mr. Seldes sagaciously points out that television executives must not fall under the spell of a false abstractionism. By this is meant that they are not to think that the "masses" form a dense, solid bloc of people which can be appealed to as one mind. Accurately speaking, there are no "masses." Society is formed of individual men beset with individual problems. Society is pluralistic in its thought patterns, not monistic. The masses must not be approached as a vast, uneducated, infantile-minded herd seeking an escape from reality or craving a thrill for the moment. The American public is not just a jazz-loving, education-fearing, shiftless mass. Mr. Seldes warns that both radio and cinema have for some time been committing suicide by becoming more and more entrenched in the false concept that the multitudes are passive, unprogressive, and undemanding. These entertainment agencies have simply created an imaginary populace. If their ideal "masses" ever were a reality, the nation would immediately become vulnerable to dictatorship. A proletariat, passive as pawns on a chessboard, would lend itself perfectly to the whims of a dictator. Television must get a fresh start, appealing to all classes which make up the social strata. Our cultural pattern must be kept fragmentized into its natural interests. Only when TV offers a variety of appeals, a range absorbing all ages and cultural levels, will that wholesome pluralism, which gives warp and woof to the fabric of a democratic society, be safeguarded. If, however, television joins with the other entertainment agencies in the pseudo conviction that the masses of the people are an irresponsible, shiftless herd, craving an escape from responsibility and life, then additional regrettable steps will be made in the direction of sheering off those diversities in our social structure which prevent the easy entrance of totalitarianism. An escape-seeking, thrill-hunting, murder-mystery-loving mind makes the perfect backdrop for the whip of the dictator.

4. *Television and problems of religious education.* Reference was made earlier to a basic contradiction in man, how that he reacts seriously to tragedy only in direct proportion to the vividness of the grief itself. Let us now relate this enigma to the problem of religious education.

The natural man's struggle with religion is curiously paradoxical. On the one hand, man realizes quite well that without personal faith in something greater than himself, he has nothing for which he can live and die. Either God exists as the guarantor of the world's values, or man is lost in a friendless, valueless universe. The alternatives are just that clear. On the other hand, he flees from religious commitment like a bounding rabbit evading the teeth of a pursuing fox. While only the law of God can prevent man from a descent to animality, the very last exercise that the natural man is amenable to take is to love God. Curiously enough, there is no limit to the effort which one will go to in insuring his other securities. Every possible legal advice is procured to insure the security of both the body and all personal property. Yet, general carelessness, or even willful obstinacy, attend the natural man when questions of soul insurance are raised. There is probably no greater anomaly in all history than this. The soul is the only thing which really counts, and yet insuring the soul is the last step which man wants to take.

Soldiers in the last war (to recall an earlier illustration) perfectly summed up these inexplicable, contradictory sides to man's nature. When all was well, the G. I. — with but notable exceptions — looked upon the chaplain as but a useless barnacle. The sooner the "padre" was scraped off, the better. To be sure, the service men stumbled over each other to attend a U.S.O., or any other show which made no moral demands upon their spirits. They loved to be entertained. It was so good for their war nerves! But when the chaplain tacked on the bulletin board the announcement of a time of prayer, no effort was spared to avoid the pain of attendance.

But, again, this was only half of the contradiction. The other showed itself when the skies were bursting with flak and the cry of enemy break-through rang through the lines. Few were the men, when death stalked the trenches, who were then unwilling to pray with their chaplain for both courage and personal salvation. Imminent death has an uncanny way of calling men back to a balanced sense of values. "There are no atheists in foxholes."

One must not censure the soldier too severely, however, for the average man on the street is no different in his conduct. While he and his family float on a wave of prosperity and health, concern for the oracles of God runs low. It is frequently only a foxhole of insecurity which forces one to reckon with more ultimate values. Material possessions diminish in value when the destiny of the soul is at issue.

There is little purpose in enlarging further on the fact of this contradiction. The problem before us is, How can television be expected to accomplish what appears to be an impossibility? How can it make men return to a sense of values when other agencies fail?

One point is the following: Television will meet man away from the crowd. Video is fundamentally a family medium. The group which gathers about it is small and intimate. This isolation is a great theoretical gain, since the more man is removed from the superficial competition of group prides, the less violently does he react to the things of God. The collusion and warmth of group life encourage an atheist. If even the children of light find it difficult to speak in public of kingdom promises, how much more do those cringe back who still lie in darkness? The natural man believes that whoever prays and confesses is simply a weakling. A self-made man would never compose confessions in the presence of others. There is a superficial boldness and manliness to the atheist's social boast that he is both the "master of his fate" and the "captain of his soul." It seems so feminine, so dilettante to require grace for strength.

When the atheist is removed from the group, however, there is less reason for him to construct such an artificial front of self-sufficiency. Social pretenses quickly dissolve when one is in his solitude. It is difficult to bluff oneself. One can feel his own heart beat. He has time then to wonder whether he will enjoy another day of life. He knows he is a dependent creature.

This principle may be illustrated in children. When they play together in the schoolyard, they make abounding claims to self-sufficiency. But when they are taken aside in Sunday School and asked to look into their own heart, they quickly confess their need of God. Adults are but large children.

This is the first point that religious educators ought to note when entering video. Television arrests man in near solitude. Thus TV, while it may threaten to convert every home into a theater, can also turn every parlor into a church. The home is a neutral area now. Whether it will become a theater or a church depends once again on both the skill and the morality of those controlling the medium. Religious telecasters therefore must be courageous, remembering that by overtaking man in his solitude TV enjoys an access into hearts which the organized church does not. Many, whose self-pride might otherwise prevent them from entering a church, may eventually find God through television. TV is an informal medium. It makes only minimal social demands upon the persons watching.

A second observation is that, since the nature of man has not changed in a television age, the emotions which man formerly sought to have satisfied through other popular mediums likewise have not changed. Radio surveys prove that listeners want at least two basic emotions satisfied when the radio is turned on. The first is the urge for *relaxation.* All people crave a change from their routine way of life now and then. We have already pointed out how TV will rise to meet this need. The second longing is for *peace.* Exhausted from the insecurities of health, finances, and social tensions, people look to religion for peace and solace. In religion they find a way in which their broken and wounded hearts can be mended by the Great Healer. Radio has supplied this need. *TV must follow in its train.*

Since partial peace of mind can be found partially in false truth, however, it behooves bearers of the truth to rally to their responsibility and produce telecasts and telesermons which meet the highest criteria set up by the industry. The masses are sheep without a shepherd. When they come to television to satisfy their craving for peace of soul, neither the TV executive nor the leaders of the church ought to disappoint them. Industry must open its doors to television, encouraging religious telecasting in every way possible. It must give technical advice to those who feel more gifted with faith than with the art of communicating it to others. Unless the American public is kept both relaxed and happy, it will not be fully equipped to face the demands of life. No television station ought to suppose for a moment that its responsibility to the public is fully executed until a proportionate TV place is given to the work of uplifting the moral and spiritual standards of the televiewer. If all work and no play makes Jack a dull boy, all play and no faith will make John Q. Public a giddish individual—one very unlike those of conviction and courage who founded this land, but one very much like the ideal pawn in the hands of a potential dictator.

5. *Problems in religious telecasting.* Because television makes its appeal simultaneously to the eye and the ear, the children of light must not minimize the skill and ingenuity presupposed for successful religious telecasting. Religion had a relatively easy time of it over radio, for all that was actually required of a program was a script and several recordings for interpretative music. If he chose—though few did—the minister could slouch

in an armchair and read his sermon. As long as his voice was appealing, he was assured some sort of an audience. The speaker could even have a bitter frown on his face as he preached on love, and if the tone in his voice did not betray a wrinkled countenance, nobody listening would be aware of it.

Television will put an end to any sham a religious broadcaster might outwardly display. The televiewer is in a unique position to evaluate both the manners and sincerity of the preacher, sizing up his contribution in terms of the TV program's total worth. Good music and speaking was all that was needed to arrest the attention of the radio listener. In TV, however, the full context of mannerism, background, showmanship, and artistry will be scrutinized by the televiewer. If the telecast sags in either interest or entertainment, a turn of the dial may swiftly replace it with a pirouetting ballerina. The season for amateurs on television will be very short-lived, indeed. Whoever among the children of light wishes to capture the imagination of the televiewers must prepare to vie with all of the dramatic wealth, talent, wonder, and ingenuity that Broadway and Hollywood can collectively combine. And that is a large order! Bids for the mind of the televiewer will become even higher as time passes. Because the medium is superior to radio in its communication potential, and because the hours in which it can reach the public are shorter by being primarily an evening medium, the purchase price of choice television minutes will be immense. The sooner the children of light become realistic about their survival possibilities on television, therefore, the sooner they will leave off their optimistic belief that an entree to video is easy to gain. In very few instances will a conventional radio show adapt itself to television without suffering a major overhauling.

One of the first problems to be faced and solved is, as expected, that of money. Here the matter is peculiar and complex.

On the one hand, staging a television series is an expensive proposition. Many religious organizations can undergird a sporadic TV production, but to subsidize a sustaining telecast week after week requires a fortune of money. On the other hand, the television industry is in a very embarrassed position so far as doling out free time to religious groups is concerned. Only the smallest of stations have begun to pay their own way yet, let alone make money. An expensive discrepancy exists, therefore, between the cost of production and the income from advertisers. This may be corrected in time as advertisers taper off their millions to radio and channel them to TV. But even then the children of light will remain on solid ground only after they have girded themselves to pay their own way on television. Programming costs will vary according to the kind of a telecast contemplated. In any case, the ones who pay their own way will enjoy the same TV security as those who advertise secular products.

Having sufficient money to finance a sustained television program, however, is still far from a full solution to the problem. TV stations will not sell choice hours to religious telecasters unless a further condition is met. That condition is that excellently produced programs back up the initial investment. The reason for this demand can be easily seen. If an oil company pays a premium rate for its nation-wide television show, for example, it wants all programs which immediately precede it to be high class. If a religious telecast, however pious its motives, drives all the listeners from the channel, it is only a matter of common sense to conclude that neither the station nor the oil sponsor will tolerate it. The strategy of both radio and TV men is to block off choice programs, syndicating them in a running series. The strategy is based on the theory that natural inertia in man will keep a channel undisturbed until the programs become unbearable. The average man wants to be entertained without disturbance, if at all possible. Television stations, hence, will be very unfriendly to religious—or any other kind of—telecasts which drive listeners away. Respect for station codes dictates that the children of light either produce excellent telecasts or stay out of television altogether.

The practical ways in which television can be used are endless. Ingenuity is all that is needed. Snappy, well-rehearsed Children's Day programs would make a homey subject. Dramatic societies can pool their talents to portray great scenes from the Bible or from the history of the church. Christian movies will naturally be excellent on TV. Cartoons can be drawn for children. Christian magic, flannelgraph work, scientific research, and band or orchestra effects will go well. And one of the most promising outlets that even a local church can sustain is to devise a telecommercial, a sixty-second drama from life which vividly advertises both the gospel and the church which preaches it. These dramas, carefully filmed, can be presented over and over just as are the advertisements for cigarettes. Through this means the gospel can repetitiously reach ears and eyes in the parlors of the nation. Furthermore, such "shorts" can be produced with a minimum of expense.

The department of religious education in every church ought to begin at once studying various possibilities of television in the program of visual education. Illustrated Sunday School lessons may soon be a standard Sunday telecast. The children of light must not be blinded to the possible effectiveness of such a weekly coverage. It might be helpful for the young people of the church partially to solve their perennial problem of keeping interest by having the group enjoy a religious telecast as part of its hour, devoting the remaining time to a lively discussion of the program's contribution to Christian thought and life. Such a use of TV would have to be carefully supervised, naturally, for an indiscriminated employment of it in the church might very quickly encourage frivolity.

No pastor ought to neglect a careful study of the church's place in television. Even if his interest be only that of counselling others, he ought not to by-pass such a duty. If at all possible an extension course through a near-by university or television station ought to be pursued.

There is one rule in television which, being so basic, must not be overlooked by whoever might seek entree into TV's new field of entertainment: *Be natural.* Appeal to the family in the home, not to an abstract multitude in the gallery. The children are there, and so are mother and father. Talk pleasantly to them. Be folksy and informal.

6. *Artistry and showmanship.* As an immortal triumph of artistry and showmanship in religious filming, one cannot easily think of a production which has surpassed Cecil B. De Mille's *King of Kings.* For over two decades this magnificent film of the Christian gospel has warmed the hearts of people. It has reached into every continent. It has been shown under every condition. The wandering little blind girl searching for the Healer, the piercing eyes of the manly Peter, and, supremely, the graces of the Master, will not soon pass from the memory of those countless millions of people who have seen the *King of Kings.* As the Master hangs on the cross, the tears flow; while in the glory of His resurrection, the heart surges with faith and hope. Because the text is faithful to the Scriptures, to good drama, and to historical settings, one can predict that *King of Kings* will become as much a part of the Easter television season as *A Christmas Carol* has been on the radio at Christmas time.

If the children of light can match the entertainment value of this highly emotional film, they will find television magnates receiving their efforts with open, grateful arms. *King of Kings* is a real audience-getter.

The first reason why Mr. DeMille's film is a rare dramatic triumph is because it did not succumb to the pious temptation to be hasty and superficial in the dissemination of the Christian message. It is a sad, but true, fact that many of the righteous fall into the fallacy of believing that, since the message of the gospel is itself so holy and powerful, it is of secondary concern whether or not one goes to an effort to be skilled in its delineation. They believe that somehow "the word will not return void," regardless how carelessly they may happen to give it out. Talented young men, for example, recently converted to Christianity, have hastily set out in the work of its dissemination without pausing for even a partially adequate preparation. "The message is far too important to be conditioned to the frail vessel who gives it out," they reason. Once again the children of this world are wiser in their own generation than the children of light. They are realistic enough to know that when the science of advertisement is in question, it is no less important how a thing is said than what it is that is said. The children of darkness sense, as many of the children of light do not, that the man on the street will pay no attention to truth, no matter how wonderful it may be, if it is not artistically presented.

This blindness of the children of light is all the more lamentable when one remembers that the importance of the message should increase, not decrease, the caution and skill by which one delineates it. The words of the king are heralded only by those briefed on the decorum of royalty, not by any rogue on the street who chances to happen along. Good diction, accurate timing, and flawless accuracy ought to be matched with a pleasing, graceful personality in all religious telecasting. Is the Master worthy of less?

A second reason why *King of Kings* is a model for TV promotion is because it is actually good entertainment. It is a rather noteworthy fact that people flock to see this film, thus showing that if Christianity were more often garbed in less offensive dress the natural man would not run away from it quite so fast. What man is there who can sit through this film and not feel a lump form in his throat when he realizes what the life and death of Christ mean both to his own heart and to the vitality of western culture?

In their sincere effort "to come out from among them," the children of light sometimes create an artificial fear of anything which even savors of being entertaining, as if by inclining to artistry and showmanship one either compromises with the world or willfully destroys the solemnity of the gospel message. Actually, these conclusions rest upon extremely tenuous foundations. If common sense and Christian decorum are respected, there is no reason whatever why messengers of redemption ought to be less skilled in the propagation of the truth than the natural man is in the propagation of error. Religion does not require one to be offensive in his approach. This mannerism is not characteristic of those who are redeemed by Christ's cross.

Quite to the contrary, good preaching ought to be good entertainment. To entertain is, as the dictionary puts it, "to engage the attention agreeably." There is no cause to think that gospel preaching should be a painful assignment, as if one is obliged to beat men with Biblical warnings of judgment as soon as he speaks. The gospel is good news! It ought to engage the attention of those hearing it just as agreeably as does the news of personal pardon engage the incarcerated prisoner. Skill and love—not challenge, bitterness, or haughtiness—must characterize the ways of those dedicated to the work of announcing to men that Christ died for their sins. Harsh and censorious manners offend, estrange, and disunite. Love is inviting, unifying, and agreeable. Who was more kind, more showmanship-like, towards those to whom He preached than the Prince of Preachers, Jesus Christ? "*And the great throng heard him gladly.*" (Mark 12:37) Since the gospel is precious to those who already believe, it should be disseminated with great skill. And since it is desperately needed by all who are yet to believe, it ought to be made agreeable, good news to their ears.

There is no need to labor the point. Religious telecasting will either be good entertainment or it will die a natural death. Nervous fingers will quickly replace a dull, Christian telecast by a less sublime, but more entertaining, feature.

7. *Decorum.* The religious telecaster must constantly bear in mind the psychological difference between the individual who goes to church on his own volition and him who by chance finds his TV set on a given channel but is too indolent to get up and change the program to another. He who goes to a personal effort to attend an organized church has made a transition from the world to spiritual things. He expects to remain in the church service until it is over. He may never come back again, but self-pride assures that he will sit committed in the entire service. In the instance of the televiewer sitting in the living room munching on an apple, relations are different. He is accidentally related to the religious telecast. There are no social restraints to keep him committed. Furthermore, a hundred and one distractions, from the wailing of the newborn baby to the cornet playing of junior, compete with the telecast. And then there is the Sunday newspaper by his side! In short, the telecaster faces no mean competition. If this apple-muncher ever suspects that he is being "preached at," he will swiftly turn to the crooning of a follies singer or a lesson in the art of playing bridge.

Televiewers want a therapy for their ills, not medicine. The person sitting in front of the television set, seeking peace of soul, is an ordinary man caught in the torrential crosscurrents of a materialistic culture. He happens to be just a man of like passions with his fellows, a man, maladjusted, lonely, and proud. He may shy away from such admissions by day, but in his solitude he confesses his need of God a hundred times or more. Such a man wants to learn in a loving way how his frustrated, out-of-line life can be straightened out and put back in shape. A bombastic reading off of his faults will only raise new defense mechanisms. The natural man would far prefer to bear his own cross than to submit to such rude analysis. A telecaster must emulate the wisdom of the devoted war chaplain. When the swearing G. I. was thrown into his company, rather than blasting away at the frustrated boy's ego and so aggravating an already bad situation, he lovingly sat with the boy, listened to his story, and then with his own tears as a solvent pointed out the way of life in Christ. Depravity may be a blinding force, but it does not for a minute destroy one's sensitivity to decency, kindness, and charity. Love, not music alone, has power to soothe the savage beast. Love is the Christian's point of contact with the world. Love is the universal song, the everlasting language of all reality. Love is a ladder of continuity between God and His creation. All speak of love. None tire of its fruit. Never has it been too abundant.

The children of light must not shun from heeding the rules for make-up and dress set down by the TV industry. The television camera can turn an inappropriately dressed individual into a ghastly, or even naked looking person on the TV screen. If the righteous, in the name of flight from the materialism of the age, refuse to abide by these standard stage conventions, they will only again encourage the proverb that the children of darkness are wiser in their own generation than the children of light.

The fundamental rules of good drama must be respected. The teledrama ought to be the most excellent piece of dramatics on the air, be it of the life of Christ or excellent Christian fiction. The Goodyear Tire and Rubber Company, which has for some time sponsored the program, *The Greatest Story Ever Told,* has set a standard for excellence and artistry yet to be surpassed in either radio or television showmanship. It is a pattern of perfection for the children of light to follow.

Theological experts must unite their best insights with those of professional script writers. Neither accuracy nor dramatics must be neglected, the one for the other. The teledrama should carry on one main plot. All characters should be introduced early, together with an early hint of things to come in the drama. All contributing action should be made evident, so that the televiewer will miss no connections. Avoid long speeches in television. Edit the plot at any point where there might be dialogue or action offensive to either taste or to racial or creedal convictions. It is evident, therefore, that either one must himself be highly competent in the field of mass entertainment, or he should solicit the cooperation and collaboration of those who are.

It is quite true that under present pressures TV tolerates the presence of many "filler" telecasts of secondary and even tertiary quality. Indeed. But the children of light would miscalculate badly if they used present standards in television as the ideal patterns of things to come. When powerful advertising agencies move into the medium with their million-dollar shows, the forum or discussion-type of program will have its relevance in TV reduced immensely. Only the fittest will survive in video!

Fear of extinction, however, is not the highest motive to guide Christian telecasting. A more wholesome driving force is a love for Christ. If the love of Christ controls a man, he will unhesitantly give his highest and best to God.

A Christian telecaster must never incline to the temptation of putting on drama or art for its own sake. A religious drama is a failure if it does not exalt Jesus Christ. There is but one gospel which men are to preach in all generations. Methods may differ in changing world patterns, but the message is the same: Saving grace, purchased by the atoning death of Jesus Christ on the cross. Such is the good news. It alone is the gospel. If TV tempts a minister to make the gospel message but a simple moral story, then Christianity itself will have been betrayed.

8. *Television and the cults.* The border cults and sects, drawing their nourishment from the emotionally spectacular, will need no rehearsal for television. These fringe groups, with their bizareness and banter, possess every ingredient for offering a pseudo religious satisfaction to those craving the routine of the spectacular: Clapping of hands, speaking in tongues, spiritual extravagances, swaying of bodies and contorting of faces in response to religious experience. The natural man, easily confusing a "religion" for Christianity, may find the spectacular of the cults extremely satisfying. Television, therefore, may increase the complexity of the religious picture. The more recognition the cults receive, the more bold their pretensions become. An extravagant faith-healing service, for instance, reaches its highest pitch only when scores of people respond antiphonally to the chants and cries of the healer. The more emotional their response grows, the more encouraged is the healer in his boldness.

Established Christianity has always been challenged by the claims of the cults and sects. Like the poor, the cults are with us always. In each generation two dozen imitations have mushroomed up about one validity. Television will increase the initial advantage which such groups enjoy over the historic gospel. The disease of "ear-itching," so noticeable in the days of the apostles, is contagious in every generation. The natural man, who loves the spectacular anyway, may become superficially more impressed by the drama of the cults than by the sober preaching of sound doctrine. Such an impression can be no more than superficial, however, for only Christ's truth will fully satisfy the heart.

As the imitations of the true gospel become bolder, however, the children of light, ever bidden to be wise as serpents and harmless as doves, must respond to the challenge with a dignity commensurate with the height of their office. Love, never hatred, must prevail, regardless how abused the truth becomes. With every increase of subtlety in the sects, the truth must counter with an even greater skill and dexterity. Christian advertising faces no problem uncommon to all other fields: The public must simply be instructed not to accept substitutes.

One cannot finally say whether TV will balance more on the side of truth or error in religion, therefore, for the future is in the hands of those who possess both the will power and the inward determination to assume leadership in the field.

9. *Roman Catholic eventualities.* When non-ritualistic gospel churches are telegenically compared with Roman Catholicism, the TV field seems to break in favor of the latter. Whereas the evangelical Protestant organism is founded on the faith that God justifies the sinner directly upon the occasion of his faith, the Roman Catholic organization clings to a sacramental system of justification. According to Roman theology, one must come through baptism, through the priest, in short, through the church as an organization. Christ continues His incarnate ministry for all time through the seven sacraments. The sacraments are visible means of grace. For this reason, and others, Catholicism has been called "the religion of the senses" and evangelical Protestantism "the religion of the Spirit."

By uniting spiritual verities with material essence, Rome easily lends itself to the new medium. Its colorful ritual is a "natural." The decorative, ornate robes of the priests and altar boys, the overlaid altar, the banks and banks of blue and red candles, the statues and images of Mary and the saints, the stations of the cross, and the magnificent and varied murals and painted windows all combine to supply a Catholic parishioner with a feeling that inside the church the eternal Christ is visibly present. When Christ's body takes on the accidents of the bread and His blood the accidents of the wine, the eternal Son of God can be literally paraded through the streets or chewed with the teeth. If a mouse found part of an elevated wafer, it would consume part of God.

From the point of view of the natural man, therefore, the Roman Catholic Church will share the same initial advantage over the religion of the Spirit as do the cults and the sects. The museum-like structure of a Catholic cathedral will easily attract more television cameras than an evangelical edifice where the parson preaches in common clothing and the faithful worship on benches purchased below cost from the War Assets Administration. To say the least, a sermon on justification by faith is far less telegenic than the visible movements in the complex ritual of the mass.

The advantage held by Catholicism in Hollywood's religious filming illustrates the point well. When the Allied States Association recently polled its exhibitor-members on what they thought was wrong with the movies, they answered, among other things, that the cinema has for too many years glorified the ritual of Catholic and Jewish religions, while doing little or nothing to make the Protestant religion clear to the nation. Yet, the American majority happen to be Protestant, not Catholic or Jewish. Pressure groups in Hollywood obtain secure places for Catholic films because of the photogenic qualities of a ritualistic religion. A nun or a monk in a habit is already identified for the movies attendants, while a Protestant has to be labeled by other devices.

World War II photography overwhelmingly favored the Catholic religion. News-hungry photographers, ever judging religious worthiness by contours and color, naturally pointed their cameras toward Catholicism, preferring an altar erected on the wing of a crashed bomber to the unphotogenic chaplain of the Protestant faith who, khaki-clad and standing in the rain, was preaching repentance to a handful of men. How could the superficial newspaper readers distinguish the Protestant service from a left-wing political rally?

Catholicism already enjoys a relatively secure place in TV. The mass has proved so successful as a standard weekly telecast in our major cities that high Roman dignitaries have had to break in to warn listening Catholics that "bodily presence" at mass is required of all who wish to fulfill their obligations to the church. While this rule of "bodily presence" may be construed as a weakness in Catholicism, the very need for the reiteration of such a rule proves that a ritualistic system is a video "natural." The mass needs no rehearsal, being part of the centuries-old tradition of the church. When full color is added to television, the ritual of Rome will take on hues of unbelievable pageantry.

Many of the by-products of the Roman system of theology lend themselves nicely to television, too. Recently in Syracuse, New York, for instance, Shirley Anne Martin, an eleven year old Catholic girl, claimed that when she kissed the head of a small St. Anne doll, just retrieved from the ash can, real tears began trickling down the doll's face. Superstitious Catholic laymen, never weary of seeking miracles, poured by the thousands into the Hawley Avenue home area in Syracuse, hoping to receive a blessing from the mother of the Virgin. The matter did not die there. Enterprising television men hustled little Shirley off to the nearest studio in an effort to make even a greater spectacle out of the incident. All were tense when Shirley kissed the statue before the television camera. Technicians testified that they actually saw tears! The incident—rich with TV appeal—was hailed as the first spiritual manifestation in television coverage.

In evaluating such an incident, one can discount at once the possibility of TV's ever being a medium to solve the perennial Catholic claim to miracles. Video is far too inaccurate in its lines to be entrusted with the responsibility of relaying fine, scientific data. TV distorts lines, changes colors, and makes dressed people appear almost unclothed.

Finally, the wealth and talent of the Roman Catholic Church adds an incalculable advantage to its credit. Vast numbers of priestly and monkish orders stand ready to respond to the slightest beck and call of their superiors, having at their instant disposal all of the stores of information in the Church's archives. Catholics will surely not rest until they have ransacked every possibility in video for increasing the security and prestige of the church.

It is well for the children of light to be briefed early on Catholic advantages, so as not to over-calculate their own securities. But there is no cause for pessimism. In the long run there is good reason to believe that the weight and bulk of the Catholic Church, so impressive at first glance, may put her at a decided disadvantage in competition with the more agile and dexterous Protestantism organism. The frozen ritual of Catholicism may be just so much ballast in the battle for primacy in television. Having pronounced a finality over its ritual, it lacks that deftness and nimbleness which must characterize a *Blitzkrieg*. Recall the pretensions of the Invincible Armada of Spain. In this incident one can see that maneuverability is an asset in any decisive contest. The bulky fleet of the Spanish Navy, with craft numbering one hundred and thirty-two and manning no less than three thousand cannons, was incontestably defeated by the spunky, maneuverable vessels of the English Navy. Because the English boats were unencumbered by such "weighty traditions," they darted in and out of the Spanish museum pieces, blowing the latter apart broadside. In quite the same relation, the Catholic Church, which insists on measuring her ritual by the changeless centuries, is always liable to be centuries behind times in adapting its program to modern moods. The mass itself may descend to pure monotony on TV.

Protestants, who believe that ritual is but a changing expression of changeless truth, can easily outflank unwieldy Catholicism in TV imagination if only they will rise to the occasion. But, contrary to proverbial utterance, this is one race which will be to the swift, one battle belonging to the strong.

In any case, one must never confuse the telegenic quality of a religion with its claims to truth. No correlation whatsoever exists between them. In the days of Christ's flesh, for example, the robed Pharisees and Sadducees were more excellently telegenic than the meek apostles who wore but the garb of the streets and whose scepter was a staff.

10. *Conclusion.* To all who join in the complex task of calling the minds of men from materialistic devotion to the things of the Spirit, a final word of encouragement is in order. Religious leaders are keenly aware of the fact that TV men have all but by-passed religious telecasting thus far. This early snubbing of spiritual truths in TV is prophetic of the long-term struggle which the children of light can prepare to face when they seek to break down the prejudice in the advertiser that only in tap dancing, murder mysteries, and banjo-type vaudeville can the public be reached. The kind of a man that such advertising seeks to appeal to is not one made in the image of

God, capable of holy thoughts; but rather a clownish animal seeking an escape from life through frivolous entertainment. The Christian refuses to believe that the best in man is being tapped when scantily dressed girls are paid to advertise shaving cream or pork sausage. Man is not an animal. He is a child of God.

It is rather self-evident that the only fully satisfying solution to the problem is for the children of light to own and operate their own television stations. If one is desirous of entering the field, he ought at once to make application for an FCC assignment. The immense costs of such an undertaking, however, will cancel out that way for practically all Christian groups.

Are there no signs in the sky of encouragement? Well, the Christian always has the promise of Christ to be with him to the end of the age and to guide and govern history for His own ends. Indeed. But there is an even less generalized comfort. History itself has something to say. The fact that we are passing through what seem to be the darkest hours in the calendar of western culture is, enigmatically, a local encouragement. War is the sword of Damocles, hanging over the heads of all. Men speak today of survival, not utopia. One of the inevitable results of such a pessimism is the puncturing of man's pride within history and the making of faith in God a more relevant alternative.

Our mid-century uncertainty and confusion is perfectly illustrated by the April, 1949 forum at the Massachusetts Institute of Technology on the theme, "The Social Implications of Scientific Progress—An Appraisal at Mid-Century." At this gathering, some of the greatest minds of our generation faced the meaning of the universal uncertainty and unrest which now plagues us. Why was man on earth? What is his purpose here? How can he fulfill that purpose best? There was an over-all unanimity on the *fact* of the predicament, but from that point diversity sharply arose. The scholars agreed on how to harness nature, but there was bitter disagreement on how to harness the worse menace, man. Man's moral problem was finally recognized to be greater than that of technological advance. Technological problems could be met by sharper minds, but who could tame man? It was the voice of Winston Churchill which summed up the conviction of the children of light. Televised straight from Boston Garden, Mr. Churchill's countenance was tense as he declared that the only hope for this, or any, generation is the flame of Christian ethics. Verily!

The symbolic significance of this forum is far-reaching. It uncovers symptoms that man's easy self-confidence is collapsing. If this be true, then that very precondition of faith, which the Christian tries to create in preaching, has set in. Humility and willingness to learn of Christ go before repentance. When the proud begin to cry for the mountains to fall on them, then it is that man begins to understand that actually there is something to be saved from. Superficially speaking, therefore, the chances of the Christian gospel's arresting the imagination of man at the mid-century are extremely good. They are as good as those of the chaplain who briefs his men just before they go off to battle. Fear and uncertainty make the security and anchorage of the gospel seem more attractive. An age of television is surely freighted with every danger. Let the righteous, after marking that fact well, courageously plan their strategy for this age.

Regardless what the future may hold for the children of light, however, they must be courageous. Whatever is not of faith is sin. Let us have faith in TV as a medium, faith in those who conscientiously labor in it, and faith in the God of history to mark out the limits of man's unrighteous pretensions.

V

Love Not Sleep Lest You Come to Poverty

In the early days of television a youthful, Southern California minister, while making a pastoral call on one of his church families, was not a little embarrassed upon his arrival to find the entire family, not in meditation or rest, but huddled before their gleaming new television set, avidly watching a full-length Hollywood movie. The incident was all the more distressing because they were the very persons who some weeks before had made the pious boast of never having gone to a movie in their life.

It was not difficult for the clergyman to conclude from this experience, and others, that the office of the pastor had taken on a new complexity in an age of TV. Whereas formerly a man could close out the world when he shut the door of his home, now the world with its good and evil, marches right into the living room and boldly takes its place beside the family hearth. The furniture in the home is being rearranged to make room for the television set. The invasion of the world into both the homes and the hearts of men has been incredibly accelerated in an age of television.

By this time the reader may have begun to suspect that the interpretation of TV, like that of life itself, is a delicate and complex assignment. There is no simple answer to the TV problem. Video is no either/or. It is a both/and. It is both good and bad, both to be praised and to be challenged. If life has complexity and mixture studding it everywhere, it is no surprise to learn that television, which boasts of being a mirror of life, also carries along with it an attending good and evil.

Having pointed out some of the more evident ways in which the new medium is capable of adding to the nation's stock pile of values, let us now study some of the outstanding methods in which it threatens to subtract from it. The reader will lack a balanced understanding of television unless the medium's full potentialities are learned.

1. *Not by bread alone.* The greatest conflict between righteousness and unrighteousness in the history of the world occurred in the triumphing over evil by the Lord Jesus Christ. When the devil tempted Christ to turn stones into bread, for instance, Christ countered with the immediate answer, "Man shall not live by bread alone, but by every word that proceeds from the mouth of God." (Matthew 4:4) The conflict between good and evil took an exceedingly subtle turn here, and few are those who have entered into its inner meaning. No outward, ethical matter was being called in question. The Lord was bade neither to commit murder nor to give His body over to fornication. On the contrary, the trial pivoted on what appeared to be simply an innocent gesture of self-preservation. Was it not natural that the Lord, who had already fasted forty days, should take food? Was it not proper for Him to be encouraged to make bread and satisfy himself? Had not the Son of God power over the elements?

The supposed innocence of these questions only makes the underlying issues all the more subtle. The tempter was after exceedingly large stakes that day. He would not have rested satisfied with the mere performance of a miracle for its own sake. Nor was the devil concerned with the physical welfare of the Son of God. His motive was wholly evil.

His interest was, rather, that of reducing Christ to the point where He would be willing to place a greater premium on His own material security than on obedience to His heavenly Father. In the counsels of God, Christ came for one purpose only. That purpose was to perform the full will of His heavenly Father. "Jesus said to them, 'My food is to do the will of him who sent me, and to accomplish his work.'" (John 4:34) In the secret councils of eternity Christ, the everlasting Son, volunteered to be the Lamb of God who should take away the sins of the world. One of the irrefragable conditions of this Messiahship, however, was that the Son, under no circumstances and by no concession, was to do other than the full will of His heavenly Father. The Son retained His supreme title, "the Lord of glory," only as long as He pursued the will of the Father. If ever His own security on earth displaced obedience to the Father, that moment His Messianic office would cancel out. Christ would then be a sinner like all men, unfit to be a Redeemer. Doing the Father's will, therefore, was an assignment of holy import to the Son. "Truly, truly, I say to you, the Son can do nothing of his own accord, but only what he sees the Father doing; for whatever he does, that the Son does likewise. For the Father loves the Son, and shows him all that he himself is doing." (John 5:19-20)

In the temptation Christ was asked to make a choice between continuing in His Messianic office or moving out on His own and declaring His independence from the will of the Father. Nothing less than these cosmic questions were called into trial. To have changed the stones into bread at the devil's behest would have been a signal to the Father that the Son was no longer fit to be called the King of kings. He would have reckoned His own physical security more important than doing the will of the Father whom He loved. He would have sinned a grievous sin.

2. *The temptation of every man.* While it is true that no man is qualified to drink the cup which the Lord drank, for only

He alone is God and man in one person, each of us is constantly being tempted to make a decision between our own will and the will of the Father. Each man is bombarded with occasions to choose between reliance on either the will of God or on bread. Sin is the refusal of man to do God's will. When bread becomes more important to man than doing this will, man immediately disclaims his continuity with God in favor of his continuity with the animals. Such a decision is sinful. Let us trace out this transition in detail.

Bread, in its widest significance, represents anything which, other than God, nourishes or sustains our being. It may be material things, such as food, shelter, wealth, raiment, transportation, or lands. It may be friends, families, social prestige, or entertainment. Or it may be the intangibilities of glory, applause, or recognition. Whatever it is, if it is not God and His word, it is bread. Bread takes in everything which pertains to earth, while the spiritual values of God include everything pertaining to eternity.

Man's glory does not lie in the area of bread. In bread-matters, man shares his table with the animals. Both man and animal crave for continuity and security within the physical world. The animal gathers nuts, and man deposits money in the bank. The animal curls up with the herd and sleeps, and man enjoys the aggregation and warmth of friends. The animal builds a nest, and man constructs himself a house. A similar pattern runs between them.

One distinguishing feature of an animal, however, is that it is completely confined within the zone of bread. This is the only locus in which it can live and move and have its being. Even the mother robin who sacrifices her life to save the young, acts on the strength of instincts which fall short of a cordial response to the commands of the living God. Animals are not qualified to worship God.

Because man may divide his time between bread and heavenly values, he may either worship God or descend to animality — depending on whether bread is given a subordinate or primary place in his affections.

It is important to note that Christ does not say that man is to disparage or reject bread. What is claimed, however, is that man is not to live by bread *alone* or *solely*. Needful bread is to be received with thanksgiving. Without bread we cannot live to serve either God or self. Christ simply commands that man should not allow himself to become an animal by making bread his exclusive diet. Man is a sheer animal whenever he lives for the accumulation, storage, and multiplication of bread. Man must not forget his origin: "The son of Enos, the son of Seth, the son of Adam, *the son of God*." (Luke 3:38).

If ever there arises an occasion when man must decide between putting God or the flesh first, one sins if he votes for the latter. Christ warns that if a man puts father or mother, sister or brother, husband or wife, children, or even his own self, before his love to God, he declares himself to be a sinner. The end of sin is death. "For what will it profit a man, if he gains the whole world and forfeits his own life?" (Matthew 16:26)

The facility with which man will forfeit his allegiance to God may be traced on every hand. All about us there are those who live and die for the increase of wealth, prestige, earthly power, social security. When gold or pleasure are in the balance, souls are auctioned as cheaply as hay or wood. The Bible, therefore, pronounces a curse upon those who, being full of earthly goods, esteem their possessions as an everlasting security. It is difficult for a rich man to enter into the kingdom of heaven because his own money vaults become his trust.

One significant reason why bread has such deluding powers is that, unlike the values of the spirit — such as faith, hope, and love — it is quantitative and measurable. One can store up his gold. He can feel the security of his good employment or a well-constructed house. A person would sadly delude himself, therefore, if he thought for a moment that bread is not tantalizing and alluring. It is hard to follow truth, justice, holiness, courage, faith, hope, and love. The course of least resistance is to live for those things which are seen. But without the eternal values which come from God, man is a mere animal. Yet, he is the worst of animals, for his freedom involves the awful power of destruction.

3. *Television's number one threat: secularization of our culture.* Of the several ways in which television may be a destructive force of the manners and morals of our culture, none rises to such disturbing heights as that of threatened secularization. By this is meant that video may make a generation of bread eaters out of us. To "secularize" is to "make worldly or unspiritual." The things of flesh may be dressed so alluringly and kept so accessible, that a chronic televiewer, deluded into thinking that man *may* live by bread alone, will sell out his divine sonship in favor of the baseness of animality. No more lethal force in TV could be conceived than this efficiency to blind men to both their kinship with God and their responsibility to live by the word proceeding out of His mouth. The efficiency of television to mirror the world in the home may swallow up any abiding concern in man to be devoted to the things of God. Broadway and Hollywood, delighted with TV's access into the parlor, will rise to the challenge of glorifying the secular. Television may repeat, night after night, week in and week out, with the tireless rhythm of the sea, that man is most fully man, not when he is lined up to the precepts of God's word, but when he is taking his ease with bread. TV's appeal is cunning. It is as subtle as any temptation. It does not ask man to kill or steal; it only commands that stones be made into bread. Like

trickles of water seeping through small fissures in a dike, television's pressure upon the heart of man may force its way through remaining resistance, until at last its power is so relentless that all opposition crumbles before it. If the children of light spend Sunday afternoons looking at Hollywood movies over television, what place will the children of darkness give to bread?

Early trends point unambiguously in the direction of TV's becoming a natural agent for secularizing the nation. Serving as sort of a clearing house for the combined talents of the legitimate theater, cinema, stock company, radio, and comedian bureaus, it is already a hodgepodge of frivolousness. Sensing the unifying powers that television offers, almost every species of entertainer is anxious to throw his weight behind the new medium. One can safely prophesy that if Milton Berle — who now reigns supreme as the number one attraction in video — can gain a Hooper Rating of eighty through his skilled coordination of memorized jokes, a volley of nonsense skits, and well-timed, barbed squelches, he will quickly be imitated from coast to coast by scores of other comedians who, somewhat slow to climb on the TV band wagon, are now quickly putting their house in order to exploit the new medium's potentialities. Milton Berle has so electrified TV listeners in many areas that on the night his show appears, theater houses detect a sharp decline in attendance, night clubs lose trade, and many shops and restaurants, not having an installed TV set of their own, close down to enjoy the frolicking Berle. In television, then, "bread and circuses" will be glorified far beyond any point ancient Rome could boast.

Unquestionably the children of light stand on solid ground when they fear a new wave of secularization in an age of television. Almost all of the features on television are, when judged by strictly legalistic standards, quite unobjectionable. Drunkenness, nudity, gambling, etc., are not the TV practice. The raucous melodrama lies on the border, indeed. But *legalistically* it also will pass. Even the Hopalong Cassidy films have a commendable moral code for the kiddies. Television's error is infinitely more subtle than such overt corruption. It does not wear its heresy on its sleeve. Its sin is covert. The trouble with TV, as with the rest of the entertainment world, is that its *whole* emphasis, its *basic* philosophy, makes no room for Jesus Christ. All problems are happily solved without any serious reference to His cross. Life can successfully be met without the slightest petition for grace.

4. *The greatest hoax in history.* It is becoming more and more evident, as time elapses, that video seems destined to play a major role in spreading the delusion that the whole man can find full satisfaction without a serious reference to God. It is quite true that one may find "better things for better living by chemistry," but it is not true that he can find the *best* things for the *best* living through this means. The eternal values of the spirit, those vitalities which neither fade nor perish through the using, proceed from the will and nature of God. By no conceivable manipulation can they be formed out of chemicals. Plastics and automatic washing machines may afford a measure of better living, but only truth, goodness, holiness, justice, and love can consummate the best living. Loneliness, a will to die, fear, pessimism, and despair of spirit are inward disappointments which can be corrected only by spiritual values. Chemistry may give us bread — for which we are thankful — but it cannot give us satisfactions in the inner soul. Only the word of the living God can do that.

Of all the hoaxes which have deluded men in history — fraudulencies which include everything from auctioning imaginary kingdoms to exhibiting concrete images as bona fide fossilized men — none has begun to enjoy the success of the empirical scientist's pretension that through the control and prediction of natural forces one can carve out a utopian civilization. From one end of the land to the other millions of people are deluded into believing that man's hope is science. Nothing could be more removed from the full truth. Man is spirit as well as body. The bread of science will never bring happiness to the spiritual side of man. As a bread eater, man is simply an animal. But no man in his right mind can be happy believing either that he is an aminal or that the end of all living is a plot of ground for a grave. Only a serious reference to God can elevate man to that position of dignity which he senses by intuition ought to be his.

Since atomic power has been released, however, scientists have become less sure of their ground. The atom bomb has been thrown into the lap of the nations. Now, realistic scientists have been obliged to concede the fact that moral forces, *about which they have nothing to say*, are actually more important, more vital, and to be more carefully guarded and defined than the laws of physics and chemistry themselves. Our generation's predicament turns on the taming of man, not the atom. Physicists are now facing the following questions: What is justice? What is the right? What is the good? What is decency? What is holiness? Science is coming to sense that unless these standards of character are unambiguously defined, the survival of civilization itself is endangered. Science is moving slowly from its diet of bread to an appreciation of the word of the living God. The movement is cautious and reluctant, but progress is there nonetheless.

This means that a new emphasis is falling on normative science, that branch of learning which defines for man what he *ought* to do. Physics and chemistry can, at best, only announce to a man what *is*. If we are to control the atom bomb, however, it must be heralded what man *ought* to be. Ethics is a normative science. It prescribes right and wrong conduct. Without its sure voice, we have no hope in our generation. Unless there are normative standards of right and wrong, eternally written into the fabric of the universe by God, then there is no meaning even to raise the question whether one ought either to kill or refrain from killing in atomic war. It will not do simply to protest that it is "inconvenient" or "socially disconcerting" to see men be killed; for there are fanatics who, taking delight in the shedding of blood and seeing an advance of social forms by the destruction of the "inferior" races, find killing both convenient and satisfying.

Scientists seem wiser than many television magnates, however, for whereas physicists are encouraging research to learn whether we can find our way back to normative ethics in this generation, TV officials thus far show little concern for the predicament of modern man. While the world totters on the brink of chaos, television programs merrily beam bread-entertainment to the world, just as if all is well and peaceful. With a persistence matched only by the egress and regress of the tides, video gluts the air waves with ball games, puppet shows, water carnivals, circuses, ancient films, comedians with a hundred gimmicks, jugglers, wrestling burlesquers, acrobatic dancers, card players, and a dump truck full of other balms to soothe man into believing that he is able to know life's fullness by bread alone. It is almost incredible that such a mass frivolity could be condoned when our civilization seems to have a prophecy of doom written over it. It is just a plain lie that man can have peace without reference to God.

If television does not permit its channels to be used for the spread of religion, ethics, and standards of holiness and justice, it may actually prove in the long run to be the worst gift that science could have put in the hands of men. It may forge the final link in the chain of modern, tragic pretenses that man is not a child of God. The word of God advises: "Set your minds on things that are above, not on things that are on earth." (Collossians 3:2) Television quickly responds: "Set your minds on the prize fight in New York City, not on things that are above."

5. *TV's first home: the tavern.* While one ought not to rest too much on the fact that the beer halls were the first to capitalize on television (for the initial costs of sets forbade average, private owners buying into the medium at once), the tavern's immediate seizure of TV in the medium's first days is symptomatic of the mind to which the new agency appeals. Historians will have to reckon with the fact that when TV bowed for its first public appearance, it found a natural environment, not in places where discrimination in social taste reigns, not in the parlors of churches or social agencies, but in liquor taverns. This very incident is a solid piece of evidence to support the conclusion that television is not directly concerned to bring men to a decision on the worth-while things of life. The tavern clientelle is made up of those escapists who, through drinking and reveling, find provisional relief from life's tensions. The menu of the tavern is "bread and circuses," only, all the day. To block out any vestigal reminders that there is such a thing as a saddened, demanding world outside, on the one hand, and to insure that the patrons will be kept cordially related to the establishment in their descent to animality, on the other, darkened windows, soft lights, sparkling fixtures, pin-ball machines, and a rhythmic juke box aesthetically adorn the room. Only the occasional tambourine of a Salvation Army lassie disturbs the serenity of those looking on the wine while it is red in the cup. Christ went everywhere preaching men to live soberly before their God; but the motto of the tavern is to encourage men to eat, drink, and be merry.

Why has television given prosperity to the tavern? The answer is that, carefully screened, video feeds a continual stream of entertainment features which make absolutely no moral demands upon those watching. Tavern patrons insist on being told that their way of life is the best. They cry, with those of old, "Prophesy not unto us right things, speak unto us smooth things, prophesy deceits." (Isaiah 30:10) The man in the tavern cannot stand having the light of God's truth penciled at him, for the judgment of God against those who take their ease in Zion is severe. The prophet preaches that the natural man is full of sin and transgressions, that "It is a fearful thing to fall into the hands of the living God." (Hebrews 10:31) Television defies this. It encourages televiewers to suppose that final satisfaction will result when one forgets his problems by laughter and entertainment.

The secularizing potentialities of TV are very subtle. One is not committing sin to watch television football. Indeed. But when he is encouraged to believe that in chronic addiction to such events, he is accenting the highest in him, sin lies at the door. The very fact that television is in harmony with the tavern's philosophy is enough to stir up thoughtful citizens. The tavern draws its crowds by dulling the senses to real life. The tavern patron seeks to gain citizenship in a make-believe world of fancy, a realm where he is free from economic, moral, and social pressures. He wants to forget the sweaty coal mine, the carping wife, the unpaid bills, and poor health. In the smoke and din of the room he tries to lose both his individuality and his responsibility. In the tavern he enjoys a collusion of like minds. This adds further encouragement to his pretension.

But such an escape is as spurious as the promises of science. Sooner or later all must be faced once more: the coal mine, the nagging wife, the debt collectors, and physical weakness. Then — if not before — man will learn that entertainment features are but an anesthesia: they only deaden, not cure, the pain.

However, one must not be too harsh with the tavern clientele. Actually, the Scriptures are no less severe in their indictment of those who anesthetize their spiritual obligations either by ruling a vast industry behind the shield of an aluminum desk or by enjoying security through a vault of money. In fact, the classic parable in the Bible to illustrate the folly and sinfulness of those who put their trust in bread is not the drunkard — much to the surprise of the respectable man on the street who glories in his self-righteousness — but the successful farmer. Yes, a farmer! He is charged with putting his faith in his large crop and his huge barns. That was his guilt. He trusted in bread to the exclusion of the word which proceeds out of the mouth of God.

If a barn filled with grain can delude a man into overlooking his security before God, how much more can television, which puts the glitter and glamour of the world in the living room, anesthetize the careless? The universal testimony of televiewers is that, despite the flaws of the new medium, they are no longer able to live well without their set. They find sitting hours in front of the TV screen is a narcotic. It is habit-forming. Only the individual who deliberately disciplines himself will avoid being lulled into the sleep of secularization. The same telecasts which dovetail with the mood of the tavern are now flooding the homes of the nation.

6. *TV's number two threat: the destruction of personal initiative.* At the termination of World War II the nation was amazed to see the works of art which war prisoners had made, waiting for their liberation. Although they had neither the tools nor material with which to work, the men somehow managed to form skillful creations. Some took discarded pieces of wood and whittled out lamps or book ends. Others made airplane models from Red Cross boxes. Picture frames, musical instruments, traps, toy guns, puzzles, and many other items of

interest were created by the imprisoned men. When hostilities ended, these items were exhibited in store windows for others to enjoy. Not a few of those watching were ashamed when they saw what these men had done with so little, while they themselves were doing so little with so much.

The real value of the works of handicraft was not intrinsic, however, for no skilled musician would abandon his Stradivarius original for a caricatured violin glued out of cigar boxes; nor would a connoisseur of fine art exchange a Ming dynasty porcelain for an inlay fashioned from pine. The deep value of the works lay in the fact that they symbolically represented a victory in the soul of the soldiers. They stood for a triumph over idleness.

Prolonged idleness began to act as a rot in the fiber of the soldier's spirits. This was the experience of the war prisoners. By doing nothing, they began to decay internally. Their morale suffered atrophy. To ward off what otherwise would have been an inevitable manifestation of living death, the prisoners stimulated individual and group initiative. They realized that somehow they had to interest themselves. Out of this determination emerged the violin and the mouse trap. By keeping occupied with such projects, an internal dissolution was staged off. Here, then, was the real worth of the inlaid jewel box or radio case: By remaining absorbed in such creations, a soldier conquered a battle within himself. By living *for* something, life itself was recovered.

Since we are all soldiers in one way or another, it is once again easy to trace a parallel between the military man's problems and those of each of us.

There are two types of people in the world: Those who only *exist,* and those who go on to the art of *living.* Let us examine these types. Those who merely exist think of life simply as a weary routine of eating and drinking. Their concern is but to keep themselves alive. They have no particular goal in life. They merely exist. Creative powers are unaccented. Many aged people lie in this grouping. They pine away under the necessities of physical existence, eating and drinking only because they are required to.

The second type is the person who, continuing very much to exist, goes on to the zestful art of living. He is creative, ambitious, impatient. He sees life as *purposeful* existence, not as a monotonous, decisionless realm where physical survival is the highest good. Such a person lives *for* something. He uses his freedom to reach beyond, to gain, to learn. Notice the way of the child, for example. Each day is a new thrill. Each night is feared, for the promises of the day are too rich to be left.

The person who simply exists, but who refuses to live zestfully, is under the same threat of internal dissolution and decay as the idle soldier in the enemy camp. The soul is like a self-charging battery. When it has vision, its vitalities are increased. But when faith fails, decay sets in. "Where there is no vision, the people perish." (Proverbs 29:18).

An ambitious person has initiative. Initiative is that forward movement in the soul by which a man goes after something. A stubborn mule, which must be driven on its way, has no initiative. A child that is bribed to eat his morning cereal lacks initiative. Initiative is operative only when people pursue a task ambitiously, creatively, earnestly. Initiative is a concerned response, an earnest desire to gain or to control. Observe the painstaking way the Pilgrims left Holland for this country. Guided by a vision which transcended local comforts, they braved storms and disease, resting only to bury their dead and to thank the Lord of the sea for mercies. They had initiative.

The value of living a disciplined life is that in and through the effort a courageous, determined will is forged. Just as physical exercise increases the health of the body, so determination, courage, and struggle, strengthen the fibers of the spirit. With each determination, each decision for the right, the soul has new strands of character woven deeply into it. This new strength in turn contributes to the future victories of the will. Henry Ford once told some of his associates that one of the secrets of his life was that of completing everything he started. Even if it was sensed that an invention might not work, for the sake of his own self-confidence it was followed through to the finish. With each success a deposit of courage was laid on the soul. Mr. Ford knew that more was at stake than just another invention. The will itself was being disciplined. That was of far greater value. He who quits loses something inside of himself. He endangers his self-confidence. He undermines future success.

Curiously enough, television, which has a responsibility to entertain men, bids fair to be so efficient in its assignment that initiative in man may be choked to death. The more television does man's entertaining for him, the less he is bound to do for himself. Even the simple interruption of a telephone call — be it from one's pastor or the local butcher shop — is a resentment to an avid televiewer who is having others do his thinking for him. TV may make lazy men even lazier.

Even in so coveted an assignment as educating the masses television will have to walk a narrow line to avoid becoming a menace to personal initiative. Excellent education makes a demand on the pupil. If a Latin teacher allows her students to write translations between the lines or if a geometry instructor supplies a book of answers with each volume of problems, such teachers are accomplices in the students' deterioration. Good education transforms the student by making him work for himself. Education is not simply the communication of facts. It is the creation of a beautiful soul through the pains of birth within the individual himself.

Television — skillfully used — *can* teach and create. It can stimulate essay contests, forums, and extension courses. That is true. Its perennial danger, however, is that it may tell men the answers without requiring any thought on their part.

Exhibit A of the early collision of television with the aversion of the multitudes to giving birth to knowledge through self-transformation is the April, 1949 showing of C.B.S.'s mystery show, *Suspense*. In the story that night the "Creeper" slew a redhead named Georgia. To afford an opportunity for the televiewer to use a little personal initiative, video men did not come right out and say in so many words who this beastly "Creeper" was. Plenty of clues were given to help, but the final decision was left to the televiewer himself. The venomous individual was really the locksmith who had just fixed Georgia's front door. The locksmith had spoken his part distinctly. But the TV audience, with eyes glued firmly on the pictures, overlooked the verbal clues. As a result, a deluge of calls descended on C.B.S.'s Manhattan switchboard. An army of frustrated "gawkers" on the other end protested that they could not sleep until they were told the answer to the mystery.

The course which television must tread is delicate. It cannot demand too much from the televiewer, or it will lose the audience. If the populace desired to go through the agony of self-transformation, they would have enrolled in college in the first place. But if TV stuffs the air waves with an endless parade of entertainment features which make no demands upon the televiewer whatever, it is difficult to see how it can *avoid* being a bad teacher. If television does everything for a man, it will become increasingly unlikely that the individual will stir up any self-activity himself. The more he has his thinking done for him by another, the less he will be interested in doing any himself. Once again television has the opportunity of creating either an enlightened proletariat or molding a mass mind to respond to the dictator's whims. If televiewers get in the habit of "letting TV do it for them," it eventually may be that they will be willing to "let a totalitarian state do the rest." This is a quick way for a nation to commit suicide.

Early reports show that television has the potentialities needed to sap initiative from the individual. One survey, for example, indicated that televiewers listen to radio 92.4 per cent less regularly; 58.9 per cent read fewer books; 48.5 per cent read fewer magazines; and 23.9 per cent fewer newspapers. Of course, this is TV's opportunity, providing it is seized. Most of the reading that people engage in is trash anyway. Still, it is not difficult to sense a danger. If people so easily give up reading so-called "best sellers" in favor of watching a marriage on roller skates over TV, will they not just as easily give up reading the Bible, the classics, and wholesome novels? It is rather startling to see a medium emerge which can change the habits of people over night. A steady, fragmentized culture is less vulnerable to mass delusion than one unified around an entertainment medium.

If it turns out that people in a television age devote less time to self-examination, hobbies, writing, music, art, and thought, our loss will be greater than our gain.

7. *First rebuttal: radio did not destroy initiative.* Some say that since radio has not jeopardized initiative in man, TV will not do so either.

One has missed the full height of television's potentialities if he thinks that a narrow parallel between it and radio can be lined up. The difference between the two mediums is immense. Television appeals basically to the eye of man; and it takes time to watch something. Radio blotted up much of our time, but video much more. One could knit, work on a hobby, clean the house, wash his car, or even study geometry while listening to the radio. In TV, however, one is called upon to give his whole conscious self to the medium. In only the rarest of instances can anything of a constructive or vocational nature be accomplished while the television set is on. Television is much greedier than radio, therefore.

Furthermore, it only requires a small amount of effort to turn off the radio and begin something else. With but few exceptions no radio program is attractive enough to compete with live activities in life. It is the exception when one sits and listens to radio without simultaneously doing something else. Radio has become our friend, and will continue so to be in daylight hours, because it is a companion to us, supplying us with sort of an orchestrational background for our work. The housewife listens to the "soap opera" while she does her work around the home. Radio keeps us from being lonely.

But television, like a new bride, will play second fiddle to nothing. It demands a full-time devotion. People who attend the movies leave everything else behind them. During the entire time that they watch the show, they expect to accomplish nothing else than be entertained. Television will make approximately the same demand.

8. *Second rebuttal*: *people will become accustomed to television*. Many contend that present correlations are premature in that they overlook the three "stages" in television watching. The first is the *novelty*. Here the televiewer "gawks" with amazement at the thrill of having a movie in his living room. He carries his food from the kitchen and eats in front of the video set. The second stage is *transitional*. In this zone the individual, still very much thrilled by novelty, yet eats his meals in the kitchen where he ought. The initial reaction is beginning to wear off, however. The final stage is *selective*. When one has had his set long enough he becomes critical of it, turning to only certain telecasts, avoiding the rest.

Since familiarity always breeds contempt, one must make the provisional concession that television's initial novelty in the home will assuredly wear off. But even after conceding this point, it must be added that the remaining question is far more complex than one might first think.

Actually, these three stages are pursued only by one type of mind. As far as the masses of the people are concerned — the uneducated bloc which makes up society — there is no hope that they will ever move to a serious "critical" stage. Such a refinement never developed in radio. The lower classes turn the radio to just whatever happens to be there. It is a depressing, but realistic, fact that the great proportion of the populace must be taught from the beginning how to use radio guides and to be critical in selection. The same will apply to television. The tastes of the ordinary man are too unrefined for him to be critically "selective" in his tastes. If jazz is on one station, he allows it to continue, despite the fact that with a slight turn of the dial he could enjoy a full symphony orchestra. The responsibility of teaching people how to use television will have to fall on pastors, concerned educators, civic leaders, social workers, as well as on those in TV itself.

But a more profound reason why present correlations are warning signs of a potentially worse threat to come is that such correlations may be *under* rather than *over* statement. Both the quality and the quantity of the television programs will increase as the industry continues to receive millions and millions of dollars of advertising support. When once video ascends to a high income bracket, it will be able to compete directly with the talent of both Broadway and Hollywood. For the moment video is losing far too much money to collide seriously with the highly paid, highly unionized talents in the centers of professional entertainment. This unbalanced economy is bound to level off, and when it does, there will not be a "star" in the country who will be unwilling to get on the band wagon.

Nationally know entertainers are slow to leap into television. For the time being they are waiting for more money. Typical is Tommy Dorsey. While admitting that TV is the greatest medium for mass entertainment in history, he yet tells news reporters: "I have been approached several times for TV, but, as I analyze it, it's too much of a job today. There's not enough money being put into programs to support a band such as mine. So, we're going to sit back for a while yet until TV really gets into the groove." Bob Hope, when quizzed by newsmen, added his philosophy on the subject: "Radio has an average of 80,000,000 listeners as opposed to about 15,000,000 who see television. Until TV is further perfected and developed and its potential audience increased, I do not plan to have a television show of my own." These judgments are typical. Television must get into the proverbial "groove." Then, alas! all will flock to draw a check on its wealth.

One of the most far-reaching movements in Hollywood today is a shift in many of the smaller studios over to the production of TV "shorts." When television can meet their prices, even the major studios will put their million-dollar spectacles at its access.

It would be unrealistic to conclude, therefore, that because certain people go through an easy cycle today, they will do the same when the medium is financially undergirded. If the present flood of "canned" films, forums, household chats, trivial piano ditties, and uneventful quiz shows hold millions of televiewers spellbound, what will be the end result when there is sufficient money on hand to produce really spectacular telecasts? It is not an impossible thought that in its full stature TV, badly managed, may increase the percentage to one hundred who read less, write less, and think less. The more lavish the telecast, the less easy will it be to turn off the program to go for a walk in the park, work on a hobby, or read a good book.

Likewise, when *color* comes to television, an immense increase in drawing force will ensue. While television remains a monochromatic medium, it only touches the outer skirts of its full powers. Every amateur camera enthusiast knows that when one has once looked at pictures shot in full color, it is exceedingly difficult to be content with those taken in black and white. Color enriches so much. It has a depth which cannot be surpassed. When television programs are beamed in full color, therefore, the resistance of the televiewers to snap off the set will shrink immeasurably.

As time passes and television becomes more skilled, an efficiency to make people better and an efficiency to make them worse will grow up together. And part of this mixture is video's threat to destroy initiative. If multitudes of people lessen their vocational pursuits, reading, and writing, watching telecasts in black and white, who will excel in personal initiative when video is beamed lavishly in full color?

9. *Religious initiative.* Since a peculiar type of initiative is required for one to sustain fellowship with his God, a word must be said about some of the problems attending this type of self-discipline.

Certain philosophers have associated religion with what a man does with his solitude. While this observation is only a part of the truth, it nonetheless is a very important part. It is a belief of the children of light that God has sown the seeds of religion and divinity in the hearts of all men, but that such seeds are germinated only when men turn to self-examination, confession, and conversion. Religion is an individual task. While many other duties in life may be performed vicariously, no one can be religious for another. God addresses each man personally. And He calls for a response in individual faith.

The Christian faith is a religion of the spirit. Quietness, self-examination before God, and solitude in prayer, therefore, are prerequisites for a healthy soul. The children of light have always been commanded to build altars in the wilderness, to enter tents for prayer, to conduct fasting and singing, and to withdraw from the idolatrous defilements of their neighbors. The Lord often retreated to the wilderness or the mountain to be alone with His Father in prayer. If the Son of God believed that initiative in religion was essential, ought not those who are sinners by nature make full use of the means of grace?

Probably the most perfect attitude of inwardness is prayer. In prayer one deliberately turns aside from the demands and distractions of the world to enjoy an intimate fellowship with God. Prayer is fellowship directed heavenward. For success in prayer one must first block out the world behind him. Otherwise concentration is impossible. One should seek a place of quietness and solitude for prayer. "When you pray, go into your room and shut the door and pray to your Father who is in secret; and your Father who sees in secret will reward you." (Matthew 6:6) When doors are shut, the praying heart makes an absolute declaration of independence from the world of animality and the bread of mammon. Christ spent the Last Supper with His disciples in the quietude of an upper room. Below them scurried the nervous world, while they sat together in calm peace.

The frenzied pace which men are beckoned to follow today is exasperating. From morning until night we seem pressed on every side to go! go! So set on edge are our nerves that we have lost sight of the blessings of relaxation and meditation. It is surely the exceptional person who takes time off to be alone with God. The resulting sin of this maddening routine of appointments and assignments is that of becoming too occupied to appreciate the words which proceed out of the mouth of God. Our diet again is bread. This is a very subtle sin. Engrossment in trivialities seems to give a superficial peace. If a man deliberately keeps himself busy, somehow he believes that he is living very fruitfully. It does not matter so much to him what he is doing, just as long as he is enthusiastically committed to an endless round of appointments.

Television may be the straw to break the camel's back. By its voracious appetite to gobble up every spare moment, the work of taking time to be holy will now be made exceedingly complex. It may encourage televiewers to forfeit their privileges of prayer and fellowship with God by jamming their time with entertainment. Formerly one had some opportunity to relax at night. But with a private movie screen in the living room, anxious to light up during the hours of the night, it will not be easy to set aside a time for prayer and Bible reading in the home.

There is really little that the children of light can do to change the course of events in history. They ought at once to reconcile themselves to the speed and restlessness of the age, therefore, determining that they will take time to be holy, regardless what others may do. Unless the children of light are going to risk having their fellowship with God endangered, they must periodically bring their speeding life to a grinding halt. Time must be taken to be holy. Holiness will not come automatically. Trivialities can rob even the enlightened of fellowship with their Redeemer.

> *Lord, I have shut the door,*
> *Speak now the word.*
> *Which in the din and throng,*
> *Could not be heard.*

> *Hushed now my inner heart,*
> *Whisper Thy call.*
> *While I have come apart,*
> *While all is still.*

If a person finds it impossible to be alone with God in the press of his home life, he ought to join with others in a spiritual retreat. This may be through the church, or it may be a private project. The author, for example, recently shared in the leadership of such a program. Sponsored by the Inter Varsity Fellowship for Southern California students who desired to be alone with their God for a few hours, a retreat was held high in the San Jacinto Mountains. With the distractions of finances, term papers, examinations, and scholarly research left behind in the valley, the students opened up their hearts to God in solitude and quietness. In the early hours of the morning each retreated to a distant point for a season of prayer and meditation. Some went into the woods, while others sat on rocks beside a singing mountain stream. But all laid bare their hearts to God. In the group assemblies the entire number jointly studied a chapter in the Bible. The leader made a specific point only to ask questions of those reading, encouraging each to give birth to knowledge in his own heart. An entire week-end was spent with God in this way. When the group wended their way down the side of the mountain to take up tangled university responsibilities once again, all agreed that new strength to live for God had been received.

Business man, housewife, and student — all ought to face their need for taking time to be holy. There is none so sanctified but what his soul is always in danger of being defiled. "Pride goes before the fall." (Proverbs 16:18) The soul is like a garden. Given proper cultivation, it can be converted into a thing of beauty and splendor. But left unkept, weeds will overgrow it, covering its delicacies. Sin encourages men to let the weeds grow lushly in their heart. The flowers of holiness blossom rarely. The loss of God's fellowship is serious, however, since only God can give man peace, happiness, and, finally, everlasting life.

10. *Sunday television.* The ordinary means by which God has been pleased to increase a fellowship in the righteous, both with Himself and with each other, is through the established church, with its rightful preaching of the gospel and the administration of the true sacraments. Television threatens even this security.

If the machinery of the television industry were to shut down on Sunday, and in so doing afford the nation an announced relief from its purveyance of bread, TV's threat to religious initiative would be lessened greatly. As it stands, however, Sunday is a video field day. TV follows the pattern set down by the rest of the entertainment world. The cinema looks to Sunday patronage as one of the most lucrative of the week. Likewise, radio men, realizing they have their largest potential audience on Sunday evening, block off their best talent for that time. In the recently publicized "Sunday night scramble," for example, in a desperate gamble to control Sunday evening air waves C.B.S. offered to N.B.C. talent the enticing bait of a mitigated federal income tax bill. On Sunday evening, therefore, radio men line up their most powerful entertainers in bloc formation. Announcers on give-away shows have half the nation anxiously hoping to make a fortune by simply answering the telephone.

Television, with its best eye on the Sunday multitudes, is bound to put its finest foot forward that day. Video will be a new menace to righteousness if it schedules telecasts designed to woo away the Sunday night church attendant from spiritual faithfulness. The children of light must take caution.

It must be made clear here, however, lest a premature misinterpretation result, that the Christian has as much right to watch television on Sunday as at any other time. "The earth is the Lord's and the fullness thereof," and that includes Sunday television. There is no more sin entailed in Sabbath television than in hearing a symphony program over the radio or in walking through the park. Television is a sin on Sunday — or any other day — only when it becomes an occasion for one to break the law of God. The difficulty with video is that it may provide the nation with a new excuse for postponing righteousness. TV will make it all the more difficult to attend to the ordinary means of grace in the church.

Some children of light look lightly upon the thought of attending worship services on Sunday night. The logic by which they defend their practice is quite faulty, however. The Bible, indeed, sets down no law that one *must* go to church twice on the Lord's Day. But for that matter there is no law that one must go to church at all. We are living under grace, not the beggarly elements of the law. Our only law is love. It is love for Christ which binds the hearts of believers to one another and to their Lord. Love is the only reason for regular church attendance. "For the love of Christ controls us." (II Corinthians 5:14). Love knows no legal bounds. It is selfless, forgiving, understanding, courteous, kind, long-suffering. A lover seeks the security of his beloved before his own. The boy who loves a girl does not tally up in a legalistic way the things he has done for her. On the contrary, after every gesture of love he attempts to devise new and more fecund ways by which to express his boundless affection for her.

In like manner, the devoted, consecrated Christian does not seek how little he can do for Christ and still be His child. Rather, the more ways he can please his Master, the happier and richer his life becomes.

The church is the bride of Christ. Faithful attendance at all her stated worship services ought to follow in response to love, not duty. Like the Psalmist, one should be glad when he is called to go into the house of the Lord. In the Lord's house love is made perfect. When the children of light turn aside from Sunday evening worship in favor of radio or television delights, therefore, they suggest that their hearts are not fully yielded to the Lover of their souls. Fellowship with Christ is maximized when one joins with the assembling together of the brethren. Love asks, "How much *may* I do?" Not, "How much *must* I do?"

If the children of light try to justify their rejection of evening church attendance on the ground that their soul does not need the added spiritual support, they only exhibit a further underestimation of the spirit's crafty foe, the evil one. Satan, anxious to have men say "Peace!" to their own hearts, could find no more subtle way to rob a Christian of strengthening graces than to persuade him that too concentrated an attention to the things of Christ is a superfluous activity. The first downward step to a defeated Christian life is to commit the sin of believing one is far from falling. If the mighty men of old have fallen, who is he that can stand forth in an age of television and declare his security? "Watch and pray that you may not enter into temptation." (Matthew 26:41)

Nothing by way of counsel can be given to the children of darkness. Believing that setting aside any portion of the seventh day for other than the self is a sheer triviality, the children of this world esteem each day alike. One can only regret that such are so hasty in rejecting God and the moral law, however, for without anchorage in heavenly things man is as hopeless as the animals. The beasts of the field regard each day alike. The price man pays for scorning God, therefore, is a reduction to the commonplace of animality. Atheists and animals have more in common than faculties for breathing. Both are unredeemed. They have come from dust, and to the dust they shall return.

VI

The World, The Flesh, and Video

1. *Video's third threat: the exploitation of fleshly lust.* In the October 11, 1948 issue of Life magazine there appeared an article which indicates another reason why television must be used with caution. In this release, entitled "First Television Discoveries," *Life* editors revealed that movie talent scouts were now able to save on shoe leather in finding potential cinema timber by just sitting in front of their own television sets. This particular account describes the early success of a TV actress who found her way to the movies. The illustrated release depicts a young, lustful, chorus girl—supposedly working her way through college—standing beside the desk of her college professor, donned in a tight sweater. She is seductively staring at the instructor, seeking, siren-like, to lure him away from his meditations to embrace her waiting charms. So the plot of the teledrama went. Movie scouts, always delighted to be put in touch with women who are able to seduce and distract men, immediately signed up the video actress for a role in a forthcoming cinema production. The hypothesis which guided the scouts was, doubtless, that if a girl is skillful enough to lure her professor from his research, a man who knows quite well the shame he will bring down on himself and on his profession by yielding to student overtures for romance, she could also attract the man in the street whose gold is so badly needed by the thirsty box offices.

One of the favorite devices of both the legitimate theater and the movies has always been that of modeling "blazing beauties" for the lustful eye of the public. Hollywood has long encouraged "leg art" among its starlets to keep the industry lush with funds. That is bad enough. But when a *public* medium gives provisional signs of resorting to the same unworthy method of retaining economic security, the very moral standards of the nation stand challenged. It is regretful that this problem should even have to be discussed at all. If ever pure and wholesome standards ought to be encouraged, the time is now, when western culture is passing through the death test of survival.

In evaluating TV's potentialities to contribute to the moral delinquency in the land, however, one must be cautious and realistic, taking pains neither to exaggerate nor minimize the actual situation as it is. Doubtless, this is an extremely difficult path to pursue, for the natural inclination of the children of light is to accent the sordid side of the medium, while the children of darkness incline to see nothing but its good. Each must learn to interpret the medium in its broadest dimensions.

2. *The most alluring form of bread: lust of the flesh.* Bread is never so alluring, never so tantalizing and pleasant to the eye, never so sweet to the lips, as when it is adorned in the foil of fleshly lust. One proof of this is the fact that great and just rulers, men who would rather have abdicated their rights to the kingdom than forfeit allegiance to the laws of God for the nation, have prostituted their dignity on the altar of lust for but a single moment of passionate indulgence. Perhaps the most convincing illustration of this is King David, greatest of the Israelitish monarchs and prototype of the King of Kings, Jesus Christ. As a servant of the Most High, David had no equal in his day. He feared God from his youth. His walk with Jehovah was so close that the resulting religious experiences, poetically set down in the Book of Psalms, have been found to be

normative reflections of man's deepest ventures with God. King David was a model of magnanimity, understanding, courage, and wisdom. His favorite diet was the word which proceeds out of the mouth of the living God. And yet, despite this lifelong walk with God, despite all of his antecedent spiritual preparations, this mighty monarch was reduced to ignominy and shame in the course of a single moment. The Holy Scriptures, realistic in their account of even the noblest of men, tell how David, walking one evening on the roof of his house, chanced to spy the shapely form of a woman bathing herself. Overtaken by the power of the flesh and forgetting for the moment the honey-like quality of the word of the living God which forbids lust, this enflamed king bade the woman be brought to him. Adultery followed. After the sin, David, like all men, immediately came to himself. The incident was a dart of shame and guilt in his soul. Out of fear of the consequences, he turned to the expediency of telling falsehoods and, alas, even committing murder itself. Surely God forgave the weeping king. But that flow of tears was quite insufficient to blot away the fact that here was a man who righteously ruled a nation but was impotent to resist a woman.

A similar declension occurred in Solomon, David's son, save that it now was more open and accepted. Sin has an effect of deadening sensitivity to guilt. Solomon, while he was skilled in building the temple of God, was unable to keep the temple of his own body clean. Because he loved so many strange women, the Lord rent the kingdom from his house.

No less monumental of the frailty of men is the account in the Bible of the fateful dance of the daughter of Herodias before King Herod. As the charming young girl shamefully pirouetted before him, the king refused to turn away his eyes; thus fulfilling the truth of God's prophetic word: "For the lips of a strange woman drop honey, and her mouth is smoother than oil. But in the end she is bitter as wormwood, sharp as a two-edged sword. Her feet go down to death; her steps take hold on Sheol." (Proverbs 5:3-4) As the charmer whirled about him, Herod's sense of better discernment was replaced proportionately by the passionate perspective of an animal, until, at last, under the drug of emotional unbalance the king rashly pledged to the girl whatever she might ask. When the dance was over, the enflamed king came to himself. But then, as usual, it was too late. The mother of the girl seized the occasion to even an old grudge, however. She demanded, through the lips of her daughter, that the king forfeit the head of John the Baptist on a platter. Herod was broken up inside when he realized what he had done, but his pride forced him to make good his vow— thus, like David, adding murder to his lust. What the king thought would be but an innocent moment of merriment proved, in the long swing of events, to be his downfall. "For on account of a harlot a man is brought to a piece of bread." (Proverbs 6:26)

3. *Concern by the children of light.* The Scriptures in no light way treat with the sin of unchastity. Adultery is included in the Ten Commandments. The later prophets warn that the wrath of God is pent up against those who defile their bodies. In the New Testament Christ raises the sin of lust to the highest power by lodging it within the inner intentions of man himself. "I say to you that every one who looks at a woman lustfully has already committed adultery with her in his heart." Matthew 5:28) The Apostle Paul says that no unrepenting "adulterers . . . will inherit the kingdom of God." (I Corinthians 6:9-10)

Perhaps there is no area of the Christian faith which is less appreciated by the natural man than the Bible's scathing indictment of unchastity. Marital infidelity is so fashionable today that those who remarry are many times viewed as "chic" and "extremely smart." Students in state-supported universities are instructed in psychology and sociology class that sexual impulses are but hypothetical situations to be experimented with as are any other data in science. As a result of this "scientific" advice, free love, trial cohabitation, and traffic in contraceptives are the universal rule, not the exception. Any presumption that God will hold a boy or girl responsible for defiling the body is decried as ancient or Puritanic. Modern man has outmoded such "credos." Outstanding comedians employ suggestive puns to maintain their security on the radio. The legitimate stage lives on borderline drama. The movie industry, rather than scorning its "stars" for their immorality, converts their notoriety into an occasion for greater box office appeal. Magazines with shocking pictures choke the drug store racks, seeking, with few exceptions, to impress the youth of the land that standards of dress and chastity are guided merely by personal feelings. In short, one is "not quite up to date" until he breaks with a philosophy which teaches that sex privileges carry along an attending responsibility.

The children of light recoil from approving modern standards. When the emotions are once given the authority to usurp the primacy of the intellect, the glory of man has departed. No one is quite so indistinguishable from the animal as he whose passions fly out of control and who lives on an indulgence of the flesh. Enflamed passions can narcotize man quicker than stimulants. Emotions corrode a man's sense of values by pleading an intense, rather than a lasting, satisfaction. So intense is the promise of sex pleasure that its momentary enjoyment is believed able to compensate for any consequences which might ensue. This promise is a lie. The temper never enlightens the indulging one of the fact that guilt, shame, loss of self-respect, and inward grief are inevitable fruits of chastity destruction. "Shun immorality. Every other sin which a man commits is outside the body; but the immoral man sins against his own body." (I Corinthians 6:18)

4. *Lust and the practice of espionage.* Sensing the simple way that sexual temptations break down moral resistance in man, military and political espionage has been quick to employ seductive, feminine charm as a very effective means to induce those in places of high responsibility to tell their secrets. Modern Soviet Socialist Republic agents, for example, maintain a skilled corps of white slaves, disciplined for the single purpose of piercing moral resistance. These female slaves to the Kremlin—who fear Stalin, not God—carry on their lethal traffic of espionage wherever official business is transacted. In the office, night club, or theater their assignment is always that of reducing men to the shame of bread.

In a less modest, but no less guilty, way much of modern life is riddled with espionage forces. Sex is used on billboards from coast to coast as major leverage to move man into doing or buying things he might not ordinarily consider if less emotional standards were followed. Magazines, handbills, transit car ads, window displays, and catchy neon signs of most every description join together in making capital out of woman's powers of seduction. When one stands at Times Square in New York City in the early hours of the evening, for example, he can pivot on his heels in almost any direction and see lust and sex glorified. This is but a concentrated glut of exactly what is going on in practically every hamlet in the country. Many of the so-called "best seller" novels leap into a place of prominence because of the frank and sordid plots which are threaded through them. Without bared bosoms modern entertainment is thought to be ineffective. Children's comic books open on the first pages with compromise situations. The plots are then launched in lust of the most base sort. And the contribution of the Hollywood film industry to the delinquency of our nation is almost unspeakable. Over a decade and a half ago, for instance, high sociologists and educators made an exhaustive study of the influence of the movies on the nation's children. Their findings were collected in a volume by H. J. Forman, entitled *Our Movie Made Children*. The book, choked with objective, scientific facts, soberly concludes that the influence of the cinema on American children is "a critical and complicated situation." Seeking to inform the public, rather than moralize against the movie industry, Professor Forman was obliged by the facts themselves to conclude that the wholesome contribution of the cinema was far outbalanced by its negative perversions. And no perversion ranked higher in his correlations than that of sex. The great movie "bloc" is made up of the youth of the nation. By consuming a fringe of suggestiveness in the film plots, these young people become convinced that practices such as petting and necking are quite normal pastimes in our society. The movies create a perfect backdrop for more intimate relations in a parked automobile.

Early television trends suggest that this new medium intends to take its place behind this espionage movement. Unscrupulous TV advertisers are already, Delilah-like using sex as a drawing force. While the scantily dressed girl had to remain motionless on the billboard, over television, as in the movies, she dances for the public view. Her purpose is to sell refrigerators, not call for the head of John the Baptist; but the method employed is just as unscrupulous. If TV continues to substitute espionage for good advertising, it may eventually destroy the science of propaganda itself. Sex is surely a short cut into the hearts of men. But the price which the nation must pay for this descent into animality is immense. Formerly, good advertising consisted in showing the *virtues* of, say, the new automobile. In video, however, a captivating model emerges from the trunk of the gleaming car and casually assures all who watch that they will be most "chic" if they buy that model. Lustful women are used to sell cigarettes to the televiewer. The motive behind such a practice is exactly the same as that behind the maneuver of the Kremlin white slaves. By stirring up the passions of the televiewer, it is hoped that an emotional response to purchase the product will ensue. Young people who watch the actress puff her cigarette, anxious to gain social prestige themselves, will conclude that the way to climb the social ladder is by imitating her. Such "respectable" espionage is merely quantitatively different from its more violent counterpart in Communism, however, since in both cases a deliberate effort is made to corrupt the image of God in man by sexual temptation. Such advertisers forget that when one company rests its case on sex, it opens the door to the loss of its own appeal by a bolder sex display in a competing product. Unscrupulous advertisers likewise overlook the fact that when they encourage men to sin, they themselves are an accomplice in the act. They will share in the guilt.

Social decay will inevitably result from carelessness in advertising and entertainment. If man is only an animal sexually, then there is no compelling reason to believe that he is responsible to the laws of truth and justice either. God's law is either over the whole man, or it is not over man at all. Why should man be responsible to God for truth and justice if he is not morally responsible? Chastity is part of the Ten Commandments, the moral structure upon which western culture rests. And if the truth of one law is called into question, then they all must be, for each and all turn for their validity upon the strength of their claim to be a reflection of the will of God for man.

The connection which holds between moral and ethical laws is exhibited perfectly by the Nazis in World War II. Having cut man loose from God on moral questions, the Nazis swiftly concluded that the state is higher than all the other laws of God, too. As a result, promiscuity in sex was followed at once by the license of idolatry, dishonesty, and murder. As mere animals, the Germans excoriated, butchered, and beheaded their opponents, and all in the hallowed name of the "Third Reich."

How modern advertisers expect to stop the nation from following the same path is far from clear. The very devices of suggestiveness of which they make such capital form the first step in the overthrow of the Ten Commandments, the laws without which free enterprise itself would be impossible. Free, economic enterprise is possible only when society respects honesty, justice, and fairness. When man overthrows responsibility to the laws of God, the decaying anarchy of class war, price fixing, unscrupulous union leadership, misrepresentation, and unjust distribution set in. Enigmatically enough, when lawlessness reigns in the land, those very corporations and centers of entertainment which so cavalierly by-passed man's responsibility to follow chastity, may themselves be the first to suffer the flame of vengeance. Mob rule will turn to the violent overthrow of capitalism when moral tension is relaxed.

Fortunate for her, America is still undergirded by a Christian heritage. A deposit of grace, laid by God-fearing men of yore, has stayed off a moral collapse on the home front. How long this residual righteousness will atone for the punishments this nation ought justly to suffer, only providence knows. A cursory knowledge of history is enough to prove, however, that no culture can long retain its initial virility when it has internally collapsed on moral issues. The organism of the nation is no stronger than the organism of the individual. When once the fiber of character is corrupted, then the whole man starts to decay.

5. *Television and the law of proximity*. The serious side of television's entrance into the field of espionage stems from the fact that it enjoys an easier access to the hearts of men than do other methods of espionage. It may thus make character decay easier. Let us examine this possibility in greater detail.

It is a firmly established axiom in moral studies that the more accessible a field of temptation becomes, the greater is the number of those who fall into actual sin. It is no particular temptation for one to steal from a bank if such a house of finance is completely inaccessible. But when one is in a position of authority in the bank and, consequently, can easily alter auditor's figures, facility in sin sets in. A child may be anxious to remove candy from a dish right in front of him, while remaining quite undisturbed about hidden bags of candy in the cupboard. Accessibility always tends to increase the surface of temptation and sin. The couple in a parked automobile enjoy an easy intimacy one with another, a familiarity of relation absent when the two sit at tea under the watchful surveillance of parents.

Since the nearer one is to temptation, the easier it is to fall, it is only common sense that a wise man will anticipate the possibility of his failures by withdrawing from areas of temptation and sin. The Apostle Paul encourages the children of light to avoid any situations which might lead to sin. He likens the gaining of heaven to the winning of a race. "Do you not know that in a race all the runners compete, but only one receives the prize? So run that you may obtain it. Every athlete exercises self-control in all things." (I Corinthians 9:24-25) If a boxer or wrestler is exceedingly fond of apple pie, for instance, so much so that he cannot endure the sight of that pie without eating a piece, such an athlete, knowing that he will break training rules to indulge, will be wise if he deliberately absents himself from places where that delectable morsel is sold.

The Christian likewise, intent on gaining heaven, ought to avoid all occasions which increase the possibilities of new temptation. One ought to choose his place of employment, his friends, and his entertainment so that they add to, rather than subtract from, his faithfulness in holiness. If the Christian fellowships with those of lewd minds, he is guilty of sin—the sin of leading himself into temptation.

Sensitive to this axiom of proximity, some have tried to solve the problem by founding anchoritic and monastic colonies in the desert. They wish to effect a complete withdrawal from the temptations of the world outside. To avoid lusting after women and gold, these men in cloth leave both behind, favoring the solidarity of the monastery. The weakness of the monastic solution, like that of most forms of total abstinence, is that it does not commend itself to the man on the street. It is a luxury which few can afford. Most people have social and financial obligations which keep them chained to this world of sin. The Christian, whether he wills it or not, must fire furnaces or paint walls beside the citizens of this world. The children of light must pay taxes with sinners, breathe the same air as they do, and march in the same war. There is no other course for the ordinary man to follow, therefore, than to do his best to be *in,* but not *of,* the world. In fact, the very last thing that the redeemed ought do is "to go out of the world." (I Corinthians 5:10)

If keeping oneself free from deliberate exposure to new temptations was difficult prior to the television age, how much more will it be now that the world itself is catapulted into the living room? Television will greatly step up the problems of Christian sanctification. With the world in the front room of the home, it will require new skill to be *in* but not *of* the world. In the days of yore one had to overcome an initial laziness before he could interact with the world. He had to dress, leave the house, and pay out money to attend an entertainment feature which delighted his senses. An expenditure of finances and time was needed to watch a roller derby or a drama. Television, however, will bring the mixture of the world right into the home effortlessly. Movies and professional wrestling matches are now easier to enjoy than the contents of a magazine in the rack. King David had to walk on his roof to have lust placed before his eyes. That required an effort. Television will cheerfully supply every home in the nation with an entire company of Bathshebas and daughters of Herodias to charm men with their dancing and singing. With the world situated comfortably beside the hearth, it is easy to understand why television's efficiency will encourage people to nourish their souls on things which ordinarily they would turn aside from if they were not so accessible. King David disclaimed lust, *until* he saw Bathsheba.

A peculiar problem which the children of light will not easily solve is that of determining in advance whether or not a telecast is fit to see. One must look at a telecast to discover its content. But in the very first glance one might unwittingly put himself in a temptation which finally leads to new, unanticipated sin. There is no easy way out. One must use caution, together with all of the sanctified common sense God has given him. If a person is faithful in his prayer life, God will give him strength likewise in times of television temptation. "God is faithful, and he will not let you be tempted beyond your strength, but with the temptation will also provide the way of escape, that you may be able to endure it." (I Corinthians 10: 13)

Without question, the children of this world will smile at even the suggestion of television's becoming an occasion for the increase of sin in men. They succeed in their judgment, however, only because their own hearts are blinded to the meaning of this life. They stand under the severity of God's wrath, and they continue to repeat, "It is well." Fearing neither God nor His law, thus, they deem it quite an innocent thing to gorge themselves on the sinful. A suggestive burlesque show is only a harmless way of extracting a little pleasure out of life. What harm can a small amount of fornication do? So they reason. In this age of atom bombs and biological warfare, it might profit the children of this age to recanvass the meaning of the nature and destiny of man. It may well be that man is more than an animal, and that his destiny can be understood and appreciated only in terms of the law of God. One must make a decision: Either man finds his worth and dignity in God, or he is a base animal. There is no possible satisfying third alternative.

6. *Another consideration*: *TV's power as a social influence.* Because of the sly way which it enters the home, TV carries another problem along with it. Video may set up social standards which are below Christian criteria and then, as a new social force, encourage televiewers to conform to them. Let us analyze this threat.

As every parent sooner or later discovers, there is no force which counterbalances the home training of children more than social tensions. A child will gladly permit the parent to dress him in a certain way, until he observes for himself that other children have different customs. From then on a new molding influence is at play in his life. The child now strives for social ascendancy. He will insist on being dressed like the other boy in the neighborhood. His long hair is "cute," until he hears the boys call him a "sissy" or a girl. If after the boy pleads to have his hair cut, he has to continue looking like a girl, the parents will only add further insult and personal injury to an already offended spirit.

Since we are all only large children, it is not surprising to discover that the influence of social competition reaches out into all life. Fashions drive women to the left and to the right, appealing simply to the social instincts of the woman. Men obey the same call. While they will be misers in private matters, spending a penny grudgingly on the care of their teeth, they will lavish themselves beyond their own income to have the latest automobile in the garage. Few there are who are not penny-wise and pound-foolish!

The urge within us to maintain social security is a compound of both natural and sinful elements. The natural is the *law of self-preservation*. This dictum is woven deep into the fabric of life. It is that involuntary bent in our hearts which gives us a fear of extinction. The law is good and wholesome, for it goads men to sustain life and to retain dignity and self-respect. This fear of death is shared, in part, with the animals. Like the beasts, man wants to live.

The sinful ingredient is *pride*. Pride converts the law of self-preservation into an inordinate force. It takes our initial urge to live and steps it up to a point where one is willing to anchor his own security at the expense of a neighbor's. A proud person wants to be equal with or, preferably, superior to, all others with whom he comes in contact. Pride perverts and corrupts the wholesome intentions of the law of self-preservation. It sparks individuals to take inordinate steps in securing their prestige.

Social competition has its bright side, to be sure. Without its power we would lose much of our incentive to make progress. It is through the interaction of social forces that history moves on to higher forms of art, science, justice. But one of the dangerous by-products of this force is the encouragement of a person to do or approve things solely out of a fear of what others will think. As an individual, a person might turn aside

The World, the Flesh, the Video   151

from sin, but when he is with the "gang," he senses a new, impelling drive within him to conform to the pattern. Children are often polite and thoughtful in the home, while showing rude and offensive manners when they chum with children of that stripe. High school boys will drink or smoke, not because they have come to a moral decision on the issues themselves, but because it is accepted by the crowd. They must either follow the crowd, or they will not be high school leaders. School girls likewise approbate the license of petting on the grounds that, though they find no thrill in it, they tolerate it out of a fear of what the boys will think of them if they stop. Adults do the same thing. Concern for social censure lashes them on to actions hitherto unanticipated. The trouble with people is that they permit pride to overtake their better judgment. They are more concerned to keep their own egoistic security than they are in maintaining common sense before God's law.

The classic example of this power of pride in social relations is found in the history of Israel. After noticing that other nations had an earthly king over them, they themselves cried for a monarch. God had promised to be their everlasting King. But the Jews, more anxious to please themselves than God, cried out for a visible king, one "like all the nations." (I Samuel 8:5) With a visible king over them, one to whom other countries could send ambassadors and official legates, the ego of the Israelites would be flattered.

As a consequence of the increased efficiency of modern communication techniques, the latitude of social interaction has vastly increased. Formerly one had only to keep up with the proverbial "Joneses." Now he must keep up with the entire world. Radio put the speech habits of people before us. Catch phrases, accents, mottoes, and jingles have spread around the world. The contagion was swift because of the craving in all who listen to be in on the latest things. The movies set patterns of morals and conduct for millions of people. As the movie "star" conducts himself, so the millions of "fans" do likewise. When movie stars make their public appearances, people gasp and clap. The fans have an almost uncontrollable urge to imitate these national idols, hoping through such an imitation that they can impute to themselves part of the glory and fame the others enjoy. Advertisers are quick to capitalize on this character weakness in the movie attendants. One who admires a movie star will likewise admire the way he lives and the manner in which he dresses. If the star smokes, drinks, and lives in infidelity, the fan will believe it vogue to follow in his steps. For advertising, hence, a beer company needs only display a favorite movie star drinking its beer — that is enough.

If radio and the cinema enjoy a power to mold the minds and morals of men, how much more will television? It unites the voice of radio with the vividness of the movies. It has the power of unifying the entire nation in one telecast. When one looks at the sordid possibilities of the medium, its potentialities are frightening. Without notice, a telecast of the life of Christ will be followed by a sixty-second telecommercial showing a chorus model reclining on an overstuffed couch, gently puffing on a cigarette. She slowly explains to the "gawking" televiewer seven reasons why she finds this brand so mild to her throat. To make the argument absolutely convincing, her fifth husband stands behind the couch winking his assent. Only the deliberately blinded can miss catching the menace that a badly directed television enterprise may encourage.

Probably no zone of social patterning is freighted with greater danger, however, than that of immodesty in conduct and dress. America has long been in the process of glorifying the Ziegfeld girl. In video a veritable cult of female worshipers may emerge. With little advance preparation and financial overhead a salacious young girl, willing to loan out her charms for a few pieces of silver, can hold the attention of a large audience. If the girl just suggestively *stands* before the TV camera, doing nothing at all, she will still draw out the lust of the heart from millions of televiewers.

Television's potentialities for corrupting the manners and morals of a nation are perfectly illustrated by *Television Francais*. Beamed out of France's Eiffel tower from one of the most modern television studios in the world, unspeakably base burlesque shows from Parisian night clubs are mirrored for public consumption. These telecasts are uncensored. Show girls, wearing no brassieres and having midriffs free, are beamed out for the French to lust upon. If this depravity is condoned in a modern nation, shall America declare herself finally free from the same declension?

When a troupe of these Parisian entertainers recently trouped across the Channel to England where the salt of the righteous had not lost all of its savor, B.B.C. required that all the girls put on improvised brassieres. With so slight modification, however, the finished dance was a sufficiently close caricature of that of the daughter of Herodias before Herod that any Briton who fears God more than man ought to have risen in protest.

Whether breasts will eventually be free on American television depends on how long Christian morals can maintain their own in the land. Until American democracy declares for national nudism, a depraved television should shock enlightened sensitivity.

The very thought of putting an outside limit on decency and indecency is defiantly protested by the children of this world. All standards which fall short of complete human autonomy are overthrown as narrow and bigoted. It is not necessary at this point to remind those who object to Christian criteria that either God is God over all, or He is not God at all. Man is either a responsible creature, or he is a type of animal.

7. *The issue of television censorship.* Television committees have been very sluggish about the problem of censorship. They fear the word "censor," but they also realize that without a check on their freedom, license in wantonness might follow among the thoughtless. A corporate responsibility binds the entire industry together.

What video will finally do about supplying itself with a code of decency is yet to be officially ruled by the industry. One can only regret that in the welter of issues and problems which the new medium must meet, that of a moral code has received such subordinate attention. Video is very undeveloped at this point. Typical of its initial immaturity is its present policy of beaming wholesale lots of resurrected, class-B films as filler programs. Many of these ancient productions, being filmed before the screening work of the Hays Office, are morally more objectionable than the lustful Hollywood extravaganza now playing in the theaters. Examples of such meccas of lust which have been presented by TV men are *The Sheik* and *The Son of the Sheik.* Another equally distressing trend in television is its blanket use of vaudeville from the legitimate theater. Comedians, fresh from the footlights, are beamed into the home employing gestures and cracking jokes suggestive more of the backstage than good art. This habit conditions people for a desire to learn more intimately and personally of the ways of such actors and actresses. It is perfectly well known how sub-Christian the stage is. Television will not correct that philosophy of life by simply warning the actors that the public, not a restricted audience, is viewing the spectacles over video. One cannot teach old actors new tricks.

One of the first rumblings in the industry to put its house in order came when TV men adopted the National Association of Broadcasters' Code. This is a hopeful sign. Other glimmerings have come from the Television Producers Association, such as the following provisional statement: "No television program shall be produced which shall tend to lower the moral standards of the viewer, ridicule any law, either natural, spiritual or man-made, or in any way violate the acceptable standards of good taste, or contradict the American way of living." This is another hopeful sign. In addition to this TV men have used common sense when the indecent comes to their attention. A typical case of this is the recently televised reunion of the Air Force Association in Manhattan's Madison Square Garden. All went according to schedule until Gypsy Rose Lee, who had been employed to entertain the men, made gestures which were reminiscent of her earlier career as a striptease. C.B.S. officials immediately saw to it that the scene faded out and the threat was passed.

Sensing the slow way that the TV industry is rising to the call for a code of decency, the children of light may tend to become impatient about the issue. There is no immediate cause for alarm. If proper measures are taken, there is no reason to suppose that the problem of manners and morals in television will not work out in a very wholesome way. The righteous ought to assist in this program, not withdraw in impatience.

8. *Interstate commerce.* One of the weightiest encouragements for believing that television will respond to public pressure for high moral standards is that, unlike either the legitimate stage or the movies, it is interstate commerce. Like radio, television takes its orders from the Federal Communications Commission. What this means to the public is that television must periodically justify its existence before this powerful Commission. If the FCC can be convinced that any video station fails in its assignment to serve the public interest, convenience, and/or necessity, it will not renew the license of the station in question.

Understanding and appreciating this fact will put added arrows in the quiver of the concerned. As citizens of the United States, it is the privilege of the children of light to make an appeal to the Supreme Court (if necessary), to prove that a specific TV outlet has abandoned concern for the public interest, convenience, and/or necessity.

Doubtless the most convincing parallel illustration of cleanliness in morals over a public medium is the standard of speech maintained on radio. While it is necessary for one to listen to vile profanity from morning until night in the subway, office, and shop, he finds on his radio programs a rather consistent verbal wholesomeness. Even mild profanity is strictly taboo. Not a few radio comedians have suddenly been replaced by organ or piano music on electrical transcriptions because they forgot for the moment that their audience was the public, not their friends at the golf club. Surely, television will do a public disservice if it tolerates a code of speech standards less rigid than that of radio. Being under the National Association of Broadcasters' Code, video should be expected to carry on radio's highest traditions.

It is true that some policies of television have been neither consistent nor praiseworthy. "Dang" and "heck", words which, while slang only, were not heard over radio, flow now and then from the lips of comedians and vaudeville actors on TV. The televiewer trusts that this standard is only provisional, and that the growing pains of the industry will soon be over. Some TV comedians have mocked death and hell. This is not only poor taste, but it is poor entertainment. Fortunately, TV men blurred out a vaudeville show recently when Deity was irreligiously invoked. If television is to be completely effective, however, it must work out a method of censuring a program before it is beamed into the home.

The World, the Flesh, the Video

In any case, one would commit a tactical error if he concluded rashly that television, like the stage and the cinema, will *necessarily* fall short of Christian standards. Because the movies are self-controlled corporations, while television is federally controlled, the two mediums lie in different categories. The movies are directly responsible only to that class which attends, not to the entire public. They seek to please the people who pay in their dollars. The legitimate theater operates on the same basis. Because its audience is selective and small, the legitimate theater thrives on suggestive plots and corrupt language. While the *public* might recoil from its offensive boldness, those who actually pay money to enter enjoy it thoroughly. Consequently, the theater continues to pitch its plots on base levels. Television, however, just as in radio, is responsible to the entire citizenry, none excepted. TV is not allowed to take into account those who may not own television sets. It cannot even ignore those who, while owning sets, seldom listen. As in radio, it is obliged to function on the hypothesis that all have a right to listen. And since all may listen, all might actually be doing so at any time. Telecasters must anticipate this. The candidness of obstetrics, for example, would be quite an inappropriate topic for television. TV must anticipate school children, the healthy and the sick, the youthful and the aged. It must consider the racial and religious problems of the land.

Let none that fear God recoil from a serious interaction with the new medium, therefore. The children of light are citizens of this beloved land, and they ought not to rest until they have done their best to ease the nation into the television age with a minimum of friction or casualty. In any interaction, however, it ought to be remembered that the positive should be pressed home first. If the commendatory and the praiseworthy are not made the stronger witness, the children of light will soon be called censorious and carping. If this reputation is ever gained, then even the wholesome contributions that the children of light might finally make will be disrespected.

If the righteous once sense the full value of interaction with radio and television programs, they will claim the privilege of making suggestions. Programs, like stations, are obliged by the code of the industry to justify themselves periodically on the basis of audience response. Regardless how uplifting a program may be, a sponsor will refuse to pour funds into its maintenance unless he is given some sort of an assurance that people are really listening. That is only common sense. A radio or television show with nobody listening is but another instance of a rose born to blush unseen. The Lord is lavish in the endowment of nature, but industry is sparing in the endowment of programs. Many an excellent program has died a natural death because of the quietness of those listening. It just stands to reason that when ten thousand letters are written to support a jazz or vaudeville program as over against one hundred for classical music, the sponsor, who wants to sell his products to people, will sign a contract with the former every time. The sooner the children of light spring to their opportunities, the sooner they will add their vote that the fine and the wholesome be sustained. Be alert to occasions of good. Whenever a commendable telecast is beamed to the home, write a card or letter immediately to the station. Let your voice be heard! Call up friends. Mention the telecast in meetings of the church. Encourage the pastor to make mention of Christian telecasts in the church bulletin, suggesting that the entire congregation participate in response. "Whoever knows what is right to do and fails to do it, for him it is sin." (James 4:17)

Should the time come when the FCC is no longer impressed by righteous protestation, having abandoned its concern for the public well-being, then only Providence can help both video and America.

9. *Qualitative judgments: a new complication.* While there is reason to believe that television, being indebted to the entire public, will rise to radio's standards of decency, the nature of TV itself is such that a note of caution must be injected. As a result of having electronically wedded sound and sight, the simple censorship solutions adapted in radio will hardly cover video's new complexity. TV is a speaking medium. Yet it is more. It is an animated screen. This accounts for the fundamental difference between it and radio.

Since radio is limited to sound waves, its message is *quantitative and measurable.* A list of slang or profane words can be drawn up which are easily avoided during the radio show. If in the unfolding of the scenario an offensive word occurs, it can be screened by editorial work. Radio men do have the problem of using right words in such a way that the wrong meaning is not suggested to the audience; but this difficulty rarely proves to be more than an inconvenience.

Video rides on light waves which are *qualitative and impressionistic.* Here is the complexity: Whereas words are easily measured, a picture refuses to be classified in any simple, objective way. All men recognize swearing when they hear it. But when can one say that a glance or gesture is suggestive? When is a posture immoral? When does dress become immodest? When once the import of these questions is understood, the reader will begin to appreciate why the simplicity of radio codes will not work in television. Let us suppose that TV defines the indecent as "that exposure which excites or elicits lust in the beholder." Who can accurately tell when such an exposure has been reached? Is it not too often true that one man's orthodoxy is another man's heresy? What morally offends some is declared to be "pure art" by others. Our purpose is simply to point out the difficulty, not settle it.

One might suggest, however, the Christian presupposition that all men have standards of decency and indecency implanted in them by nature, and that these criteria, when sharpened by written revelation in the Bible, are a sufficient, practical guide for men. The closer a man draws to Jesus Christ, the more sensitive his heart becomes to holiness, and the less easily will he be apt to give the questionable the benefit of the doubt.

In any case, it is as clear as fresh cellophane that one cannot make an easy transition from radio to television and conclude from the gesture that TV's problems have been met.

There is no difficulty in movie censorship which television does not likewise face. As a result of the pressure of concerned organizations, motion picture companies recently banded together and formed a self-governing board to censor movie efforts for the entire industry. A document was drawn up to serve as a guide, bearing the following title: "A Code to Govern the Making of Motion and Talking Pictures." This code, controlled by the Production Code Administration of the Motion Picture Association of America, Inc., embodies a very excellent attempt upon the part of the movie industry to line up to the innate sense of good taste and decency characterizing enlightened human nature. The code is an honest effort to interpret the responsibilities of the industry. This is its strength. The weakness of the document lies in the section dealing with "A Uniform Interpretation Thereof." At this point an unsuccessful attempt is made to fill in the gap between the defining of decency and the recognizing of it when it comes along. It says, for example, that "excessive and lustful kissing, lustful embraces, suggestive postures and gestures are not to be shown." Granted. But according to what standard (apart from Christian sensitiveness) shall one learn when kissing *is* excessive and lustful? Is it correct to conclude that from one to five kisses are vogue, while from six to one hundred are immoderate? And when is a posture suggestive?

That the industry has fallen far short of a "uniform interpretation" of the code, is proved every day by the corruption which decorates the front of theaters and is paraded in magazines. The most lustful of postures are condoned as decorous. The existence of "The League of Decency," a Roman Catholic counterpart in Hollywood to the Production Code Administration, gives further proof of the fact that it is infinitely easier to draw up a code of morals than to interpret it in a uniform way. There is little question in the minds of the children of light but that movie censors are guilty of *under* - not *over* - vigilance. Since base dancing and drinking scenes are approved every day by the Production Code Administration, there can be no other conclusion that the whole censor attempt in Hollywood is a gesture of reluctance, not of concerned, moral response. The risque is constantly injected into plots and scenes to insure that box office receipts are sustained. A perfect case to sustain this suspicion is the September, 1949 tirade against film censorship hurled by producer Sam Goldwyn. Speaking in Los Angeles' Hotel Ambassador, Mr. Goldwyn blasted away against "petty, small-minded, single-tracked dirt-sniffers," those "arrogant, dictatorial censorship boards" who seek to put a check upon that realism which the movies wish to maintain in an effort to recapture the waning adult audience. Even the Production Code itself fell under his scathing indictment. The basic argument of Mr. Goldwyn was this: Since other mediums — newspapers, magazines, etc. — are free from censorship, the films ought likewise to have the same liberties. What Mr. Goldwyn overlooked is the simple fact that two wrongs do not make a right. *All* public mediums ought to match standards of public conscience. If they will not do it voluntarily, they must be coerced — newspapers and magazines included.

10. *A new mixture: optimism within pessimism.* The complexity of the video pattern once again leaves those interpreting it with a mixed feeling of hope and anxiety.

The hope springs out of a remembrance that television, being interstate commerce, is subject to the will of the entire public. For this reason television (other things being equal) may never tolerate the moral looseness of the cinema. An alert public can guarantee a wholesome television flow.

The anxiety grows out of several problems. *First,* since it is no easier to censor television shows than movie film, and since television is no more intentionally dedicated to the propagation of Christ's gospel than are the cinema magnates, it would seem to follow that censorship work in video will never be attended by complete success. *Second,* the voracious appetite of television will sooner or later drive video men into a permanent alliance with Hollywood studios for the production of films. There is little question but that the average television station will beam from sixty to ninety per cent of its telecasts in the form of movies. Films are to television as recordings are to radio. They are portable, repetitious, and economical. For this reason it is difficult to see how the children of light can avoid the conclusion that telecasts, like movies themselves, will, despite all, have to be classified as "good," "fair," and "objectionable." Two things equal to the same thing are equal to each other. *Third,* public opinion is a woefully unpredictable phenomenon. Although it has the privilege of seeing that television toes the line, there is no way of telling whether or not it will ever avail itself of this high privilege. Familiarity may again breed contempt. Public pressure, like the ebbing and flowing of the waves, is fickle and changing. One minute the public will rise up in wrath over a slight injustice done to someone, while the next moment carelessly approbating another war. Nazi Germany illustrates the ease in which a people can strain at a gnat of justice and swallow the camel of injustice.

11. *Conclusions*: *a call for righteous vigilance.* The children of light would make a regrettable mistake if, sensing the dark side of television's threat to the manners and morals of the the nation, they concluded that passive resistance ought to characterize their attitude. In a live democracy a concerned, interacting minority can often effect more changes in public opinion than a sluggish, disconcerned majority. If strategy and skill are kept in balance, the children of light may yet outflank the opposition in the conflict ahead.

Every effort should be made for an organized effort in interpreting television trends. One ought to recall at this point the well-known tale of the father and his seven sons. Desiring to sharpen for them the truth that a kingdom divided against itself cannot stand, the father called his sons together. To each one he gave a small twig, explaining that the piece stood for the strength of each lad individually. Then he broke each twig one by one. This was to show the ease with which they individually would be defeated. Next, he made a fagot by tying seven twigs together. The fagot could not be broken. Seven small twigs united to make one strong fagot. The fagot represented the collective powers of the sons — if they would remain united in their purposes. The principle holds perfectly true in TV matters. If the children of light collectively unite their TV convictions, they can move the world. While their individual voices might mean very little, their collective mind will not easily be subdued.

Power should be corralled first on the level of local initiative. Those among the children of light whose eyes have been opened to the promises and the threats of video ought to assume the leadership of local committees for discussion on the topic. General TV interest should be coordinated with plans to promote

Christian telecasts. After local groups are organized, a national committee might be appointed. The purpose of this national unit would be that of coordination and integration. The clubs across the nation ought to be united by a common creed, name, and organ of life. By belonging to a national society, the individual will realize that he does not labor alone in the cause of understanding and interpreting the medium for our generation. The creed ought to contain the faith of the members that, being aware of the pledges and threats of the new medium, they will devote themselves to the work of making the good of the medium triumph over its threatened evil. A suitable name for the club might be the *Teleleague*. Seminaries, Christian Colleges, Bible Institutes and other sister schools of learning could easily serve as intelligence centers for the *Teleleaguers*. The best of Christian talent ought to be combined with the warmest of Christian enthusiasm.

In this united effort to have a voice in the policies of television, however, only spiritual weapons may be used. The *Teleleague* must never become a new form of power politics, a sort of "righteous lobby" by which demands of the children of light are squeezed through the powers that be. *Teleleaguers* ought to resort only to good argument, based on calmly reasoned facts. A democracy is founded on the faith that men who are shown the right will also respect that right.

VII

Delicate Roots Require Tender Care

1. *The fourth threat of television: warping the minds of our children.* In an earlier connection mention was made of H. J. Forman's volume, *Our Movie Made Children,* a book in which convincing data are advanced to prove that many of the moral, language, and dress habits of our children are controlled directly by the movies. In an age of television, however, the worst may be yet to come. Who may predict what one will read a decade or two from today in the volume, *Our Television Made Children?* A. Gordon Nasby, writing in *The Christian Century,* remarks, for example, that the "child with a television set will see more gun-toting in one year in television movies than his parents have seen on the screen in a lifetime." Mr. Nasby's words rest on solid ground. The Western-type movie, beamed to the home specifically for the children, is loaded with guns, dynamite, and murder.

Because they are actively in the process of moral and intellectual growth, children are a special problem. Adults easily cast off impressions which a child absorbs and imitates. The cortical areas of the brain are maximal in their receptive powers while one is young. Children are little blotters, learning and retaining very quickly. The mind of the child is supple and flexible. It responds to stimuli with a facility generally unenjoyed by one in advanced years. Now, if the developing child surfeits himself on television, it is easy to see why video standards may become finally his standards. This could be serious.

Sensitive to the ease with which little ones' minds can be corrupted, the Christian church has compiled powerful, doctrinal catechisms of the faith for the children to memorize. Their language is simple and vivid. A child may commit to memory an entire catechism in the time that it takes an adult to master a few questions and answers.

In the secular field the ability of children is just as amazing. In homes where skill is used by both parents in the instruction of their offspring, it is not unusual to find the children fluently speaking German, French, and English while still in the early grades. When a man neglects his self-development in childhood, he often pays for his crime with a lifetime of regret. In matters of learning, man has his day of grace. The spirit of learning does not always strive with man. Many graduate students struggle to memorize languages with a labor equal to that of smashing rocks. What they now work hard for, they could have gained almost automatically in childhood.

If he is supplied with sufficient tools of learning, therefore, a child faces no theoretical end to growth in knowledge. Incessantly, the child poses question after question: "Why are we going to town?" "Why isn't daddy coming?" "Why?" "Why?" "Why?" And an alert and patient parent will (within reasonable bounds) do all he can to increase the child's receptive capacity. This is especially true in the case of alerted Christian parents, for they realize that if their children do not learn answers from them, they will in turn gain answers from the world. What is not faced and solved in the home may be learned in the gutter, behind barns, or in the high school shower room. One does not block the child's processes of absorption by refusing to help him. He only forces him to resort to other sources. The mind of the little one is like a stream of water: If it is blocked at one point, it either bursts the dam through its relentless pressure, or it flows around the obstacle by finding a new out-

Delicate Roots Require Tender Care

let for its power. Unless the intellect of the child continues to grow, the child will not be normal. God has so arranged life that only in activity and opposition is there growth. It will never do to crush the child's ambitions. That will only dispel life itself. Rather, the child's interests ought to be channeled and developed.

Because it constitutes such a perfect outlet for satisfying the child's ever-growing curiosity, television may eventuate into a serious menace in the development of children. Until they are mature enough to judge the nature of the world for themselves, children compensate through imitation. They imitate parents, friends, teachers, and any and all who are capable of stimulating their imagination. Children feel their worth best when they fancy they are "just like big people." By imaginatively living beyond their own age, they satisfy an inward craving for social security. Here, then, is the crux of the difficulty: Television may suggest unwholesome standards for the children's lives to be patterned after. When the puppet show is over, the minds of the children will be absorbed in a Western film. Then comes a roller derby, a professional wrestling match, and, finally, a cartoon. What opportunity will the little ones have to imitate other than the world when the viewing of one telecast is immediately followed by the plea, "Just one more?" If one will study the facial expression of children watching television for a moment, he will see the intense way that the imagination of the little ones is aroused by the experience. Every muscle in the face becomes tense and concerned. Grade school teachers already have sounded the official alarm that over-stimulation from television is being detected in the lower grades. Because the imagination of the children is tapped so easily, their tendency is to be more empathic than they ought at such an early age.

One need not be a sensationalist to sense that there is no easy way to define the multitudinous ways in which television can corrupt the minds of children. Sadistic beating, the criminally sordid, shooting, and strangling in television movies are flooding the living room. A child will be discontent to look at crime in comic books when it is enacted before his own eyes on television. A new company of television "stars" are bound to emerge from video's power to capture the minds of the children. These new heroes and heroines will then influence the morals, speech, and dress habits of the minors. And so it goes! Where is the end?

Probably no sadder illustration of the stimulating powers of television can be cited than the October 16, 1949 "mercy" killing in West Los Angeles. Left by their parents, while the elder ones were dining out, Richard Elliott, age fifteen, and his brother Robert, age ten, were given over to the tender care of the family television set. The harmless movie would surely keep the boys from getting into mischief. It was Sunday night. The boys were watching a Hopalong Cassidy movie. As the blazing of the guns sent the blood surging in their veins, Richard went to his bedroom, took a gun from beneath the mattress, and brought it back — so he testified to police officers. He wanted to demonstrate for his little brother the "kind of gun they use in the West." He was playing with his sawed-off .32 caliber gun when the firing chamber was tripped. Robert was shot in the head. The little one writhed and moaned on the floor. Testifying that he was unable to see him suffer so, Richard backed up and, with a mixed feeling of mercy and cowboy courage, fired a second shot into the head of his brother. The little one died from the wound. His pains were over. Observe how subtle the corrupting power of television is. It teaches our children to believe that gun-toting is smart and chic. Every high school boy ought to have a gun! Television says so!

Hopalong Cassidy says so! This unspeakably tragic incident ought to warn American parents that simply because their children spend nights before the video set, instead of roaming the city alleys, they are not thereby exempt from corruption. They overlook the simple fact that TV will bring the alleys right into the living room.

Little will be gained by drawing up a representative list of the concrete ways video may spoil the manners and morals of the children of our land, however, for the most important thing is the principle. And the principle is clear: TV enjoys a distinctive advantage in teaching little ones. It may instill the meaning of a materialistic culture years before they reach the university. That much is sure.

But before censorious parents commence justifying themselves by the well-used, but trite, "I told you so" formula, let us swiftly turn to the more profound side of the delinquency issue.

2. *The profound cause of delinquency in children.* At its worst, TV can only be charged with being an indirect cause of juvenile delinquency. While it may be the *occasion* for such declension, the really deep and profound cause of child failure is *parental* delinquency. Normally, only that child who has first been neglected by his parents is enmeshed in the tentacles of secularism. A parent who is faithful in the training of his family can rest in the promises of Scripture that God will take care of such little ones when they are older. "My Father, who has given them to me, is greater than all, and no one is able to snatch them out of the Father's hand." (John 10:29)

If, therefore, a father or a mother is under the fond delusion of supposing that either television or the comic books is the real cause of juvenile delinquency, he had best rethink the seriousness of the situation. The care of the child lies in *parental* hands. Only after they themselves have neglected systematic, spiritual training will the mind of the child in turn be corrupted by the evil one. *"Train up a child in the way he should go, and when he is old he will not depart from it."* (Proverbs 22:6) To conclude that TV will necessarily corrupt children is as fallacious as concluding from the fact of the falling rain that the children will necessarily get wet. Is it any less impossible to teach children the proper use of television than to give them instructions on remaining under shelter until the rain storm has passed over? Children are not mere stocks and blocks. They are free spirits. They are docile, pliable little souls into whose hearts the benevolent Creator has planted a congenital respect for parental discipline.

Many efficiently organized Christian families have already found television a real blessing. But they have arrived at this enviable relation only after giving deliberate instruction on the relation between TV and Christian morals. Others must follow in their train.

If the critical Christian parent is honest with himself, he may discover that his provisional dread of video springs more from a fear of his own teaching responsibilities, than a dread that the medium will corrupt his children. A professed fear of television may be but a cover for the deeper worry: that of having to be alert to parental discipline. Rather than being willing to pay the price of being vigilant, parents often blame a medium. The sordid in television will sully a child's imagination only after the parents themselves have first been spoiled by the sin of indolence.

To be sure, there are some cases where children seem to go bad even after the parents have been meticulous in the means of grace. They, however, are an exception to a well-established rule. A rule is responsible only for what is normal and regular, never for what is exceptional. The pervading thought in the Bible is that, given the full means of grace, God will see to it that a child's heart is regenerated by the Spirit. God is pleased

Delicate Roots Require Tender Care 171

to work in families — families conscientiously united around His word. Television may never be a scapegoat, then. While it may make corruption easier, TV's hands are tied until the knife of parental indolence cuts the knots and releases them. Juvenile delinquency can set in only after parental delinquency has gained strength.

3. *The fact of parental responsibility.* Since there are no few parents who are dulled to their own obligations, it is necessary to start our investigation at the very beginning.

Of all the gifts which God has showered down on man, none is so precious and valuable, yet so mysterious and demanding, as little children. From the simple union of the sperm and the egg there develops an organism which is so precise and complex that it makes all man-made instruments appear trivial. The preciousness of the little child lies in the cunning way its personality is forged with weakness and need. The parent sees himself in the child. This fact has given encouragement to the saying that the child is a "chip off the old block." A more accurate version of this platitude is, as one has put it, that the child is "a chip off *two* old blocks."

This is the first glory of the parents: They are creators together with God in the birth of the child. Only through the physical union of male and female is procreation possible.

However, this is only the beginning of the story. Into the hands of the parents a more grave responsibility has been entrusted. The over-all physical and spiritual growth of the child has been committed to their care. To assist in this gigantic task, the Almighty has joined together instinct and moral sense for the one project.

Instinct teaches the parent to care for the physical needs of the child. Even the hardest of men lovingly respond to the pitiful cries of a child in distress. Instinct also teaches the parent to make provisions for the intellectual and social securities of the children. A wise parent will use every means possible to locate friends, an education, and successful employment for their children. No normal father or mother will deliberately deprive the children of those things which make life on earth pleasant.

Sadly enough, however, this does not end the story of parental responsibility. When it comes to the most important office in the home, that of *spiritually* instructing the children, the average parent is woefully indolent. The powers of sin have blunted an instinctive response to holy obligations. One almost needs the famous lamp of Diogenes to locate those parents who, in this television age, are half as concerned with the spiritual texture of their offspring as they are with the children's physical and social well-being. While many a father labors diligently to insure that his family is bountifully supplied with the bread of this world, it is the very rare one who exhibits an interest in the spiritual welfare of his own. He will buy wagon loads of bread made with flour. Indeed. But the bread of the Spirit, he refuses: God, His law, prayer, repentance, goodness, holiness, salvation, heaven, and other goodly values.

This is the deadlock: The average parent easily convinces himself that when the physical and social securities of his child have been met his duty to the child is quite over. From then on the little one is on his own. This attitude, however, is really the worst sort of parental sin. Actually, the work has hardly begun. Thus far, such parental activity has presupposed only that the children are animals, creatures whose natures are fully satisfied with the bread of flesh. Squirrels care for their little ones in nearly the same way that many parents do. However pious or sincere a parent may be, if he teaches his child everything but the way of life in God, he acts as if his child is only an animal. "Seek *first* his kingdom and his righteousness, and all these things shall be yours as well." (Matthew 6:33) When a parent inverts this order, seeking first the bread of this world, he then is an accomplice in the delinquency of his children. While serving the little ones' physical and social needs par excellence, he neglects the most important thing: the spiritual walk with God. Because they are born in sin, children will no more seek after the righteousness of God without nurture and admonition from a God-fearing parent, than they will increase in physical well-being without food and water. Spiritual virtues, without which man is worse than a beast, must be cultivated with care: love, holiness, justice, charity, forgiveness, kindness, honesty, fidelity, piety, humility.

While it is true that God will ultimately require every parent to give a full account of the deeds done in the body (since each shall appear before the judgment throne of God), history itself is yet not without its own forebodings. There is probably no greater grief a parent can suffer on earth than to discover too late that the bread of the flesh is less important than the bread of the spirit. Sincere guardians, having done everything for their children except the one thing needful, have had to sit back and watch their offspring initiate a fearless rebellion against God and His law. The healthy body and the college-trained mind were turned to fornication, murder, and other unspeakable social corruptions. A parent who neglects the heart of a child may, by that very child, have his own heart broken. All of the felons in prison cells were once bouncing baby boys and girls into whose eyes hopeful parents looked. The anxiety of the parents to see to it that these children were given "everything in life" blinded them to the provision of spiritual and eternal values. When a child in the home is led to believe that he is no more than an animal, how can parents meaningfully expect him to be other than an animal in college, in sex relations, and in the business world? A periodic visit to a federal prison is one hard way some parents learn that it is far more important that the spirit of the child be kept healthy than that the body be strong. A healthy body can be converted by a sordid spirit to vicious ends. But if the body is weak, a strong spirit can create a magnificent cathedral of character, one to which men in a dark and shaky world may look for solace and guidance.

4. *The naturalness of parental authority.* To what other agency than the parents could God entrust the spiritual welfare of the children? The child has a natural fear of the parent while the parent has a natural love for the child. Tender questions of the spirit are easily exchanged by those in love. Natural instinct encourages the child to repose in the judgment of the parent, while a similar instinct teaches the parent to be tender to the children. The relation is absolutely ideal. Nowhere in the entire world is a law of respect more perfectly framed than in this relation between children and parents. So implicit is the trust of the small child for his parent — a trust that he will probably never again duplicate in later, social relations, and which he struggles to imitate even in his fear of God — that the very words of the parents, lovingly but sternly spoken, are law in the ears of the offspring. Even if the reasons which support parental decisions are logically or factually faulty, the child, satisfied with the words, will rest in them. What college professor would not delight to have such a power over the minds of his students!

Children later become very critical. Their initial obedience and docility are soon replaced by a self-reliance in the world. Whether or not a respect for parents remains at this later time depends how effectively parents have trained their children in the first place.

Since this spiritual bond between parent and child is the strongest of social relations, it is only natural that God, speaking through Moses, should command parents to make instruction in righteousness a thing of great concern: "You shall teach them diligently unto your children, and shall talk of them when you sit in your house, and when you walk by the way, and when you lie down, and when you rise up." (Deuteronomy 6:7) The most important things in life are always entrusted to the most qualified custodians. In the case of instructing children, parents enjoy this honor.

Parents are thus the logical ones to teach their children, because of the love that they instinctively have for their own. A mother will thrust her own arm into the fire and have it burned, rather than see injury come to those she loves of her household. Love never wearies. Love does not withhold from the beloved those things which are required for happiness. Will a neighbor, the church, or the school take the same personal interest in the discipline and admonishing of the child in the ways of the Lord as a dedicated and devoted parent?

Yet, is it not inexplicable to see millions of parents deliberately withholding Christ from their children in their enthusiasm to supply that bread which perishes in the using?

A parent who neglects instruction in righteousness cannot conscientiously say that he loves God, for a lover will faithfully perform whatever the beloved commands. "If you love me, you will keep my commandments." (John 14:15) Will not one willingly sing the praises of his beloved to all with whom he comes in contact?

If he deliberately keeps from them the things of God, a parent cannot even conscientiously profess a sincere love for his own children. To love God is the thing the children need most. It is their only hope, their only peace. All agree that when parents keep earthly bread from their children, they are guilty of desertion; but who senses the seriousness of deliberately holding back the bread of life? It is no trifling matter, to say the least. If an earthly magistrate requires that justice be done, will the God of heaven and earth demand less? "Whoever will not hearken unto my words which he shall speak in my name, I will require it of him." (Deuteronomy 18:19)

Many of the finest traditions in life are preserved by family ties. The art of making fine glass and tooled wares, for example, has been handed down generation after generation. Wherever this closely knit tie between families has been broken by carelessness, the particular art in question is lost. In the economy of God this same principle of hereditary teaching is followed. Families who know the things of God "should make them known to their children; that the generation to come might know them, even the children that should be born; who should arise and tell them to their children; that they might set their hope in God, and not forget the works of God, but keep his commandments." (Psalm 78:5-7) Law is law. If one will not trifle with the federal government when it comes March 15th for the payment of the income tax, will a man treat lightly his obligation to bring up his children "in the discipline and instruction of the Lord?" (Ephesians 6:4)

5. *Television and parental delinquency.* When one tries to explain why so few parents are diligent in instructing their children, the only satisfactory answer is laziness and the sin of pride. There is a congenital revolt within men against spiritual things. The course of least resistance is to talk about the weather, crops, and tomorrow's major league ball game. By carefully steering the conversation in the direction of topics cordial to the interests of the natural man, one retains his own egoistic security and pride. Perhaps the most vivid illustration of this universal aversion in man to pursuing holy things is the fear one has of giving an apology to an offended person. While an innate sense of law assures one that the only satisfying course for him to pursue is to go right to the person and offer an apology, the drag of sin within us proposes rather that

the obligation be blotted out by our becoming engrossed in other pursuits. By having our attention swallowed up in other projects, it is easy to kill remaining interests in the things which really count in life. Man's genius is remarkable when it comes to finding excuses — especially when they are needed to avoid attendance on matters pertaining to the word of God.

Over-activation, as we observed earlier, produces its own brand of "peace of mind." Therefore, whenever one desires to blunt the voice of conscience which calls him to be responsive to God's will, all he has to do is to glut his waking hours with secondary and diversionary interest. These will give their own type of peace. Overactiveness has a subtle way of narcotizing a guilty conscience. The doped conscience will come to itself sooner or later, indeed, but until that time the individual is quite at ease.

Disciplining children is a moral activity not unlike offering an apology. It presupposes real effort, for one must probe into the inward state of another personality with spiritual overtures. It requires facing issues which the children would natively prefer to leave untouched. It uncovers topics with sensitive overtones, exposing them for analysis. Taking children aside and talking to them about the things of Christ, therefore, takes courage. It is no work for a coward. It demands fortitude of will. Yet, the trouble with most parents is that they are *moral* cowards. Men gladly face the mouth of a cannon for social glory, but they wilt in fear when moral decisions in the home must be made. While it is the privilege of every parent to create a moral rock of Gibraltar in the hearts of their children, this privilege, like that of offering an apology, is availed of only by those who themselves enjoy moral fortitude.

No great acumen is needed to see why television may become a perfect outlet for the sin of overactiveness. It bids fair to be a cause of new delinquency in the home simply by encouraging both parents and children to become so occupied with trivialities that the lasting values in life are by-passed. When a parent is about to muster together courage to teach Bible stories to the children, a telecast of the life of Benjamin Franklin will tip the balances in favor of putting off that spiritual exercise. Our natural inclination toward evil gives us a momentum in the direction of negligence. Television may supply that last push needed to make the declension decisive.

6. *Complicating factors.* There are several reasons why training children in the way of holiness presupposes a special type of spiritual initiative. *First,* the time of the children is at a great premium. So full are the waking hours of the little ones that even the very thought of sleep is bitter to them. They want to be going, going, going. Now, when television's endless stream of eye-catching entertainment floods the living room, will not new complexity result? Will a child be impressed with a study of the life of Christ when the television set is beaming a Hopalong Cassidy film? The telecast is real. It is presentational. It is lively and visual. Christ, thus, will seem very far off to the child who is not skillfully dealt with. Young minds may think the messages of the Bible bookish, uninteresting, and unrelated in comparison to the action and brawn of "Gorgeous George." Parents must be shrewd and sagacious if they are going to break the monopoly in the home which television threatens to set up. If it has formerly been difficult to sit quietly with one's own kiddies, how much more will it be when television stands ready to gorge every evening? Television will snap up the children's interests the moment they leave their out-of-doors playthings and hold them until the little ones are obliged either to go to bed or to study school lessons.

Second, another initial handicap to be overcome is the cute and cunning way that a child tries to influence his parents. Children are small and weak. Therefore, they try to command certain powers over the parents. They plead tolerance and tenderness, when they ought to receive discipline. It is only too true that a parent can often be coaxed by the children to give his consent to matters otherwise not approved. This factor will make breaking with television for prayer all the more difficult. "Please?" the kiddies will cry. "Just one more telecast!" This may lead to another, and still another, until the entire night is gone. Then where is the family altar?

To make an already bad situation even more distressing, much of modern psychology sides in with the child, encouraging the parents to believe that if their children are only left to express themselves "natively," they will develop talents which might otherwise be frustrated by parental inhibition. The children should enjoy entire freedom. So, the tale runs. Such a philosophy of pedagogy runs diametrically counter to the Christian conviction, however, that "Foolishness is bound in the heart of a child; but the rod of correction shall drive it far from him." (Proverbs 22:15) If a child is left without bit and bridle, he will become a wild colt, quite useless to society. Children are born with inclinations to pride, self-will, and jealousy which must be dealt with.

Third, the *legal neutrality* of most video releases will make it difficult to train our TV children. If flagrant and flagitious sin were beamed into the home, both parent and children would easily see TV's threat. But the subtlety of a disguised secularization and an undermining of personal initiative can be detected only with shrewdness. What may be forgotten, as wrestling matches and puppet shows take the place of devotional interests, is that time is being consumed which ought to be spent developing the inner life of the child. This development should include instruction in Christianity, hobbies, schoolwork, playing musical instruments, and improving general reading and speaking habits. Television, however, enrapturing as its telecast may be, cannot, and ought not, be permitted to replace the creative, self-initiative of the little one himself.

7. *Summary.* This, then, is by far the greatest menace that television can become in the home: By being a perfect excuse for overactiveness, the medium may encourage such an excessive preoccupation with trivialities that vigilance in kingdom matters may be choked off. The threats of television to contribute to the moral delinquency of the child rank far behind this danger. The (average) child can be corrupted only after delinquency has first overtaken the parents themselves.

Modern parents have already earned the reputation of being very anxious to "get rid" of their children. Almost any strategy is followed so they can have times of peace and quietness around the house. On Saturday and Sunday afternoons countless millions of children are sent to the movies, simply that they might not be on hand to require attention. The movies "baby-sit" the children cheaper than conventional sitters. What the parents overlook, however, is that in their anxiety to get rid of their children, they may be putting the souls of their very little ones on the auction block to be sold to the highest bidder. "Be sober, be watchful. Your adversary the devil prowls around like a roaring lion, seeking someone to devour." (I Peter 5:8) It would be lamentable if television should become a chronic baby-sitter, gouging out of the child's life those hours of time which the parents should fill with initiative and direction.

Before the parent indiscriminately hands the child over to the mercy of the television set, therefore, he had best take inventory: Is his child just an animal, or is he a creature made in the image of God? This is the issue. If the former is true, then nothing matters: television, morals, life, or death. If the latter is true, then the child's soul is far too valuable to be carelessly exposed to a philosophy of secularization. A very simple law is in operation here. If seeds of holiness are planted in the child, a lovely, God-like character will grow. But if the weeds of secularism and worldly trivialities choke out spiritual interests, it is inevitable that the fruits of waywardness and perversity will fructify. "Be not deceived; God is not mocked, for whatever a man sows, that he will also reap." (Galatians 6:7) It is rather late, is it not, for a parent to weep over a child that has come to mature life? A farmer who has planted a certain type of crop must be content with his harvest. And so must parents!

8. *The issue of total abstinence.* While there assuredly is no ultimate solution to the problem of parental-child delinquency other than regeneration through the grace of Jesus Christ, yet several meliorating and subordinate considerations may be listed.

If there are cases where it is felt that television's threats quite outbalance its promises and pleasures, and a decision is made to exclude the medium from the home altogether, others ought to respect these convictions. Some will doubtless choose total abstinence. But that is their own private concern. Each man must stand or fall before his own Master. After all, television is not the most important thing in the world. The greatest question is the heart's condition before God. In matters of television, let each man be thoroughly persuaded in his own mind.

A higher solution for the general Christian mind is to treat television in the same way that he would everything else in a mixed world. Because the entire universe is freighted with good and bad, a righteous individual will not expect perfection in it, but will, rather, extract the good and dedicate it to God, while spurning and shunning the evil. This, doubtless, will be the final attitude of the Christian mind when video is as universal as radio. Those who reject television on moral grounds will be as scarce in years to come as are those today who refuse to use radios. The argument of the enlightened Christian is that, since the earth is the Lord's and the fullness thereof, anything—television included—can, and ought, to be received by man with thanksgiving. Television is a decided mixture. So, like the radio, automobile, magazine, or newspaper, it can be used to glorify either God or the flesh. The usage is controlled by the inner intentions of the user. TV is just another form of money. *Money*, according to the Bible, is not the root of all evil. No. It is the *love* of money which corrupts. Christianity teaches men to hold their money lightly, lest it become their god. So, it is the *love*, of television, not TV itself, which is our problem. What is to prevent a Christian from turning off the television set if the objectionable commences? This surely is a morally virtuous solution, for it is achieved by the inner strength of the individual himself rather than by such a paltry mechanical means as that of not having a set at all.

Furthermore, total abstinence is wasteful. It is a signal that the righteous have abandoned a strategic area to the enemy. The Christian is responsible for what he does with all of God's gifts. To surrender them to the enemy is surely a gesture far removed from good stewardship.

Before parents hastily prejudice their case against television, therefore, they ought to consider some of the objections to the solution of total abstinence. The following are typical:

First, unless the children are extraordinarily cautioned in the things of life and death, an unhealthy isolation from life's realities may develop. A chronic danger of the children of light is that of sheltering their children too much, of believing that only by a complete withdrawal from the world will there little ones be kept pure for Christ. This principle does not always work. In fact, the withdrawal practice threatens to destroy one of the fundamental laws of growth. A sapling becomes a mighty oak after years of tension and struggle. Only after many triumphs over wind, cold, and rain is it able to stand the really violent encounters. In like manner, the spiritual muscles of the child who is controlled and sheltered too much may become soft and undeveloped, unable to withstand those hurricanes of temptation which are sure to assail the moment he leaves the shelter of the home for the world. History is full of sad stories of children who, after being excessively sheltered in the home, have outraged the image of God within them the very moment they faced the winds of temptation. Paradoxically, the very parents who refuse to teach their children how to resist temptation may become new accomplices in the delinquency of their children. It is well and good to prevent children from taking poison; but it is not good if the poison bottle is not identified for the children, so that they can tell it from candy when they are alone in the medicine closet. Wise parents must methodically instruct their children in the art of resisting sin. Knowing how to flee from the devil is an accomplished skill in itself.

Second, there is probably no simpler way that children can be taught how to recognize the mixed character of the world than through a survey of the good and bad telecasts which pour into the room. One cannot deliberately take his children into the dark corners of the world to watch its crooked ways, since it is never wise deliberately to look for evil. Curiosity will only be aroused in the minds of the little ones. Prudent Christian parents should explain evil as it lies naturally in the world, thus turning the edge on the criticism that the Christian glorifies his Lord by being negative or critical. Since God pronounced nature good from the beginning, evil must be indicted as the parasite, not tolerated as the host. Television is an absolutely perfect medium for instruction. The cost of a journey through the world is small, and the results obtained are extremely gratifying. With no one around to interfere with the intimacy of the moment, parents and children may gather together in the living room to discuss TV cases of good and bad, right and wrong.

Parents who do not appreciate this observation ought to rethink the entire matter. None are so deluded as the parents or guardians who disbelieve that their control over the child will some day come to an end. Every bird either learns to fly for itself or it dies. Life works that way. The sooner parents become serious in teaching their children to fly, therefore, the less likely will there be tragedy when a transition to the world is finally required.

Third, a home which rejects television on religious grounds might stimulate a needless feeling of inferiority in the child. Television will soon be as commonplace as radio. The *savoir faire* of the Christian child may lag behind if he is not allowed to enjoy an intelligent interaction with those inventions found in the homes of his school chums. School teachers will speak freely of the merits and demerits of a teledrama, recommending this telecast and that for all the children to see. Friends will chat about their television sets in the lunch halls and cloak rooms. If a Christian child has a negative attitude drilled into him, the effects upon his total personality may be far-reaching. Self-righteousness will inevitably set in. A segregation from normal fellowship with others will then follow. The final step may even be fanaticism or, alas, a nervous breakdown.

Fourth, television can unify home interests. This must not be overlooked. The TV industry purposely spends hundreds of thousands of dollars each year to provide clean and wholesome telecasts for the family. The gesture ought to be appreciated. Few parents begin to spend nearly enough actual minutes with their children in play. The television set, by holding the attention of both parents and child simultaneously, will make the task of sitting down with the little ones much easier. Who can resist the stupid ways of either Doody, the Lucky Pup, or Muffin? Television can make home fellowship natural. The teen-aged girl may find the video set a new center of interest. Friends will discover the medium a fruitful point of rallying. The lost art of family fellowship may be restored partially by TV.

It is true that this unifying force may eventually become a detriment. Family companionship around Beanie, the plastic marionette, may tend to displace the family altar. An artificial unity around a secondary center may emerge as an excuse for spontaneous fellowship and friendliness when the TV set is off. This is the constant danger. In this life, every good is accompanied by a concomitant threat. Such problems must never finally offset theoretical blessings, however. Otherwise progress will be impossible. Everything must be used with discretion and prudence. This is a mixed world!

In negative terms, the lack of television in a Christian home (unless careful counter-measures are taken) may lead to a premature breakdown of family unity. A child who is refused a set in his own house will promptly wander to the home next door where there is one. And if this visitation is likewise forbidden, the frustration of the child will be stepped up. The wider the gap grows between the child's interests and the things he is permitted to do in the home, the more likely will be a final rupture in the serenity of family fellowship. Children have a phenomenal way of remembering frustrations and harsh treatments encountered early in life.

Fifth, total abstinence is a hard way out of the problem. Since the medium *may* be used to God's glory, the children will not easily be convinced that they are unjustified in having one. And if the children are dictatorially forbidden to have a set of their own, they may only have curiosity interests stirred up to watch the medium underground. Out of the very effort to reduce the threat of the world in the life of the child, therefore, a new interest in worldliness is aroused.

9. *Concluding advice.* Before terminating this study of the relation between television and the home, it is well that a minimal, practical program be set up for all who earnestly want to follow sound counsel in TV issues. Little advice, to be sure, can be given to those who reject Christianity. They understand neither the seriousness of the welfare of the two cities nor the possible contribution of television to that struggle. The world is their home and pleasure is their god. But to those who, fearing God, sincerely want to make their time count most for His service, the following counsel may prove beneficial.

First, because the possession of a television set is a luxury, not a necessity, parents ought to be cautious to set a sound financial example before the children. One ought never go into debt extravagantly for television. If money is spent on video which ought rightfully to have purchased food and shelter, the gesture is sinful in the eyes of God as it is foolish before men. God will look with sore displeasure upon any home having a television set when the children's food and clothing are inadequate. "If anyone does not provide for his relatives, and especially for his own family, he has disowned the faith and is worse than an unbeliever." (I Timothy 5:8) Take your time. There is no cause for rush in buying television. Both the quality and quantity of telecasts will increase as time passes. Furthermore, prices are bound to be lower—especially in color television. Children should be taught to contribute part of their allowance money for the purchase of the video instrument. If they are half as anxious to have the set in the home as they seem to profess, they ought to be persuaded to assume some financial responsibility in its ownership.

Second, after the set is installed in the home, it would not be out of order to prove that television is your servant and not your master, by planning a short service of dedication. This should be done with care. Pray for God's care and protection. In the act of dedication one publicly declares an ownership-transfer of his property to the Lord. Children ought to be Christ-conscious when they turn on the TV set. Jesus is near them—nearer than father or mother. To please Him, one must neither see nor hear evil.

A suitable formula to be recited is the following: "To Thee, everlasting Father, we dedicate this television set. Be pleased to protect it, and all who use it, from evil; and may its presence in the home increase our comfort and happiness. If ever we forget this covenant with Thee, remove from us this treasured set and in its stead place sorrow."

Third, when the TV instrument is in working order, parents would then do well to study types of telecasts. The purpose of this provisional surveillance is to gain an initial, intelligent sweep of video's total offerings. Then, independent of the children, mother and father ought to agree together on what they think is suitable and unsuitable for their little ones to see. After this, the entire family should gather from time to time and, as equals, engage in a friendly discussion about the Christian view of the new medium. It might be well to have these discussions at the dinner table. This will eliminate using up more precious time. During the actual discussion, a wise parent ought to lead the others in forming their opinions, rather than legislate his conclusions upon them. Pivotal questions should be posed. All members of the family—from the youngest to the oldest—ought to be encouraged to participate. Some sample questions for father and mother to ask are the following:

What is the purpose of television? What is the good of television? What may be the evil in it? Would Jesus have owned a video set? What should a Christian do about TV on Sunday?

This indirect approach to the problem is bound to be difficult, to be sure, but it is the only effective way to teach. Caution at the beginning of TV's history in the home is far to be preferred to regret in the end. An ounce of video prevention is worth a pound of cure any time.

Fourth, after agreement has been reached by the parents on how much television viewing the children may do and still keep up school work and family devotions, they should then permit the little ones to feel their moral worth by choosing their own telecasts. The purpose of this strategy is to let the children experiment in principles of righteousness by making sample moral decisions for themselves.

Since the children will have to make their own decisions later in life, anyway, parents ought to initiate sound teaching methods in the home. Father and mother may be surprised to learn how wisely their children will select their telecasts — especially when the little ones know that their number is limited and that they have complete responsibility in their selection. Children enjoy having their worth recognized, just as adults do.

Fifth, after the little ones have made their choice, let them go ahead with their fun. However, try now and then to sit down with them and watch the telecasts they have chosen. This fellowship and mutuality of interests will not only increase confidence in the children, but it will give the parents a first-hand coverage of exactly what the little ones are seeing.

At this point one must discipline himself to avoid the mistake of jumping to his feet and snapping off the television set whenever something objectionable appears. Always remember, when sitting with your children, that they have chosen their programs in good faith. To frustrate them after they have conscientiously made a choice is as discourteous as it is dangerous. It is discourteous, because it jars the spirit of the children. It cuts into the entertainment which they have just been promised. And it is dangerous because it is an extremely blunt way of telling them they are not capable of making good judgments themselves. The prudent thing to do is to sit with your children through the entire program. Neither you nor they will be corrupted by one telecast. What ought to be done is this: Take a mental note of your exact objections, making these problems part of your agenda in the next discussion period. Then, skillfully direct your questions and answers in such a way that the children are made to see for themselves the evil. Avoid charging them directly with being bad. They will resent it. Instruct them in the truth, and they will respond according to the truth.

Sixth, since experience reveals that people generally do things more easily when they are given rewards, parents ought to keep the privilege of watching television a premium for faithfulness in family prayer and daily Bible study. Agree with the little ones that when they are too busy to talk with God, they are too busy to listen to Beanie. Enforce this relationship! An agreement ought to be had among all on the time and place of family devotions, even if such devotions be but short prayers after the evening meal. It ought to be understood by all, that when interest in television becomes so great that one can no longer pause to pray, it is time to give TV a rest.

The danger with this, naturally, is that a legalism might result. As in feeding a new baby, have a schedule, but keep it flexible. Use sanctified common sense in applying the rule of "no devotions, no television." If it happens that there is a very popular telecast which comes at the same time agreed upon for devotions, one which the children are anxious to see, do not succumb to the pious conclusion of supposing that your children will be putting the things of flesh before the things of God if you give way to the telecast at that time. Simply have your devotions before the telecast. Make the little ones give in at some other point for this new privilege. If you have your devotions at the same time, as popular telecasts, "do or die," you may find your devotional life becoming mechanical. God respects the heart, never the times or the seasons when a man elects to come to the throne of grace. Learn to trust your children's intentions. If you are skillful in giving liberties, weaving them in with spiritual values, your children will respond with liberal interest in devotions. To hold prayer during a favorite telecast will only encourage little minds to wander.

In all cases, have your devotions with the children when they are fresh of mind. Extended television will inevitably weary them. It is not practical to have devotions after an evening of TV, therefore. An irritable child is in no condition to think about the calming of the Red Sea by Moses. Send the child to bed.

Seventh, if a situation should arise where gentle suasions fail, parents ought not to hesitate to use more severe disciplinary means. Chastening is an expression of love, not abuse. Through the use of the rod a parent may turn a wayward heart into paths of peace. In later life the children will look back upon your chastening with respect and love. "Correct your son, and he shall give you rest; yea, he shall give delight unto your soul." (Proverbs 29:17). If TV becomes lord in the house, turn it off. Its rightful place is that of servant. God is the Lord of life.

Be cautious even in this, however. Chasten — indeed. But then be swift to forget and to forgive. If the sun is permitted to set on your wrath, the new sin of offending the honor of your children may result. Restore in full honor those who have been chastened. Since this is the way our heavenly Father deals with us, it ought likewise to be the method we deal with our own children.

As a final, over-all word of advice, parents ought to be cautioned against the temptation of believing that video is our modern generation's only concern. Actually, television is but one added problem. TV threats to the well-being of our children are no different from those found almost every day in the schoolyard, on Main Street, and in the cinema. Vigilance in TV matters, therefore, must form but a small part of the broad concern a parent has for the entire habit-life of his child.

The enemy of our souls could find no more beautifully timed, cunning device than to urge Christian parents to become so enveloped in television's problems that they overlook the other serious ways in which the souls of the children may be devoured by this prowling lion. In any successful warfare, all exposed fronts must be protected simultaneously.

Christians need not fear the outcome of life in this mid-century period of atom bombs and television. The struggle for the maintenance of righteousness will be difficult, yes, but a righteous end is always in sight. "Be of good cheer, I have overcome the world." (John 16:33).

VIII

The Vertical Reference

A rather competent reader, into whose hands an early draft of this volume chanced to fall, offered the following opinion of what he had read: "While the study as a whole is interesting, nonetheless it seems to suffer from the serious defect of leaving the reader frustrated. For example, when I study the arguments in favor of television, I feel like having TV sets installed in every room in my house. But when I turn to the case against the medium, I want to throw away the one I already own. Is there not something missing here? Some link: I find two unreconciled emphases."

If all the readers of this small work suffer from the same frustration, the purpose in writing has been vindicated. The book was penned to nettle people into critical thought, not make them peaceful. The effort may modestly be compared to that pursued by the Athenian sage, Socrates. He was known as the "gadfly of the state," signifying that his task was solely that of irritating people into the discipline of self-examination. He incited the indolent to action, on the one hand, while deflating the pretensions of the ambitious, on the other. His method was to ask questions. He believed that the proper locus of all virtue is the heart of the individual himself. So, in like manner, no final gesture is here made to harmonize the diverse data which make up TV's complexion. Rather an effort is only put forth to stir up the critical faculties of two types of readers: *First*, pessimists who see nothing but evil in video. Looking at the medium through perfectionist glasses, such individuals feel justified in washing their hands of the entire matter. Against this type of mind, positive arguments in the defense of television have been detailed. *Second,* chronic optimists who, viewing video through rose-colored glasses, perceive nothing but good in the medium. This species of mind refuses to interact with the threats of TV. Against such an oversimplification, reasons why video has evil in it have been suggested. Both pessimist and optimist must recall the universality of the category of mixture.

It is well that people remain frustrated on the video issue, for only then will they be in a favorable position to judge for themselves whether the medium shall be servant or lord of their lives. No person may legislate for another what either ought finally to do with video. Each person must be firmly persuaded in his own mind. Each must come to his own decision. No individual may be held responsible for the *fact* of television, but he surely is responsible *for what he does with the medium.* Having pointed this out, the duty of the interpreter of TV has been met. Decision is left to the reader.

Let us conclude with the following observations:

First, the tension will be broken once men fail to respect fine degrees of good and evil, truth and error in history. This warning applies to both pessimists and optimists. The children of light must never become so endeared with changeless truth, absolute goodness, and perfect beauty that they lose an appreciation of, or become easily irritated by, the mixed character of history. And the children of darkness must never become so engrossed in relativities that they lose sight of the fact that man is worse than an animal apart from the eternal standards found in God. History without the eternal archetypes is chaos, but the eternal archetypes without history are an irrelevance. Without the sure guide of God's word, we have no ideals to strive for; but a guide which does not assist in the solution of our everyday problems is of no value in history.

It is easy for the righteous to condemn history as wholly wrong, even as it is simple for the unrighteous to claim that history is altogether right. No particular skill is presupposed to be a tabloid thinker. Any fool can cry, "the whole is perfect" or "history is hell." But it takes a skilled person, one endowed with great patience, penetration and insight, to tease out carefully the complex strands of good and evil which are interwoven into history's fabric.

In video matters, therefore, the children of light must be skilled. Since TV will remain a mixture of good and evil until the end of time, the righteous must dig in for a long struggle. But regardless how extended the conflict may be or how wide a front the enemy has opened up, the children of light must never forfeit the dignity of their offices of prophet, priest, and king. As prophet, they are to interpret video for Christ's glory. As priest, they are to dedicate the medium to Him. And as king they are to rule over it for His glory.

Second, the children of light will remain realistic about TV only as long as they retain this frustration: an optimism within a pessimism. A controlled tension is the healthiest state for the mind to remain in. Once the individual ossifies on the TV question, the next step is to be either unwarrantably optimistic or unwarrantably pessimistic. One must remain wholesomely frustrated. Each night he must recanvass the data. Each day his concern must be renewed. Christians ought to be optimistic about their interpretation of television, but they must remain pessimistic about the possibility of ever converting the TV industry through their work. The truth belongs to the children of light. That is their hope. But part of that same truth is that history will never capitulate to righteousness through human effort. Scripture warns that good and evil will be part of the structure of history until God decrees an end to time.

Even *teleleaguers* themselves ought to take heed. They will be defeated the very instant they allow their zeal at having the truth to be converted into an optimism that they can easily redeem history with that truth. If a person supposes that purifying television will be a simple assignment, he ought to reassess the seriousness of sin. Pride is rooted deep in the hearts of men. The *teleleague* will have to fight self-pride from its very inception. Every "holy crusade" is compounded with strong overtones of sinful egoism. When a man thinks that the cause of God rests upon him, he is in a perfect condition to succumb to self-infatuation. He may be "proud" the mission of deliverance entrusted to him is so immense.

Therefore, in all TV interests, one must cultivate a wholesome tension. An optimism about the righteousness of the cause ought always be tempered with a pessimism about the hope of redeeming history through such a means. Any state other than inner frustration may lead to either left or right wing extremes. These are critical times.

Third, one must understand that the only vitality which can strengthen a person to struggle for the right, especially when history fails to vindicate his efforts, is the grace of our Lord Jesus Christ. The Christian is asked to do what seems to be impossible: He is commanded to stand against the whole stream of unbelief. How can he continue in this gigantic enterprise? The only answer is *grace*. Because he has first been loved by God, the individual now responds to God in love. Whatever the Redeemer requires of him, therefore, he is glad to perform. God supplies the strength.

Part of the commission of Jesus Christ to His redeemed is that they bear the gospel message to all the world — including the television industry. The labors of love are light. When a man sincerely loves his country, for instance, he is willing to die on the field of battle for that nation. When a man loves his family, he will labor his entire days to ensure their security. And when a man loves God with all his heart, he will respond to that love with an entire life of devoted service to Christ and His kingdom. And this takes in TV vigilance, too. It will make no ultimate difference to him if his TV efforts are completely frustrated within history, for he serves God, not man. Knowing that his efforts are on the side of the right, his pleasure comes from doing that right.

This, then, is the vertical reference: Response motivated by a love for God. Only the vitality of grace will strengthen and fortify man to carry the banners of righteousness triumphantly. Love will never fail. Only love can bear one up through the defeats and triumphs of a serious TV interaction. The abrasive frictions of the sands of time will never outwear this vitality. "Who shall separate us from the love of Christ? Shall tribulation, or distress, or persecution, or famine, or nakedness, or peril, or sword? . . . Neither death, nor life, nor angels, nor principalities, nor things present, nor things to come, nor powers, nor height, nor depth, nor anything else in all creation, will be able to separate us from the love of God in Christ Jesus our Lord." (Romans 8:35-39)

www.ingramcontent.com/pod-product-compliance
Lightning Source LLC
Chambersburg PA
CBHW062039220426
43662CB00010B/1573